Student Course Guide
for

RANITA WYATT
Dallas County Community College District

Dallas TeleLearning
Dallas County Community College District
R. Jan LeCroy Center for Educational Telecommunications

Worth Publishers

The Design and Production Team

Economics Content Specialist: Ranita Wyatt
Student Course Guide Revision: Bonnie Harllee
Instructional Designer: Janice Christophel
Project Director: Craig Mayes
Producer: Ken Harrison
Course Development Consultants: Gus Herring, John Pharr
Media Content Assistant: Brenda Wilson
Telecommunications Information Specialist: Evelyn J. Wong

R. Jan LeCroy Center for Educational Telecommunications

Provost: Pamela K. Quinn
Vice President, Distance Education: Jim Picquet
Director of Product Development: Bob Crook
Dean of Financial Affairs: Dorothy J. Clark
Dean of Distance Learning: Edward C. Bowen

Student Course Guide ISBN (10): 1-4292-4008-3; (13): 978-1-4292-4008-6
© 2009 by Dallas County Community College District.

All rights reserved. No part of this work may be reproduced, stored in a retrieval system, or transcribed in any form or by any means—electronic, mechanical, photocopying, recording, or otherwise—without the prior written permission of Dallas County Community College District.

Requests for permission to make copies of any part of the work should be mailed to:

Dallas TeleLearning
9596 Walnut Street
Dallas, Texas 75243

Printed in the United States of America
First Printing 2009

Worth Publishers
41 Madison Avenue
New York, NY 10010

Contents

To the Student v
Course Organization vii
Course Guidelines ix

Lessons
1. The Study of Choice 1
2. Confronting Scarcity 11
3. Supply and Demand 23
4. The Business Cycle 39
5. Measuring Economic Growth 51
6. Aggregate Supply and Demand 61
7. Economic Growth 73
8. The Nature of Money 81
9. Financial Markets 93
10. Monetary Policy 103
11. Aggregate Expenditures 113
    Appendix—Aggregate Expenditures 123
12. Fiscal Policy 131
13. Schools of Thought 139
14. Economies in Transition 147

To the Student

Dear Student:

You are about to begin a course that will challenge you and encourage you to look at everyday events in an economic perspective. Macroeconomics is a look at the economy as a whole, which requires that we look back in history to see how events and past actions have influenced where we are now. This Student Course Guide integrates the textbook and video lessons to help you meet this challenge and successfully complete this course. Pay special attention to the reading assignment for each lesson. Some of the lessons contain material from several different chapters.

The video programs are documentary style, incorporating experts from academia, business, and government entities from across the United States. These experts bring to life the theories presented in the textbook. You, as the owner of scarce resources, as a consumer, or as a business person, should recognize many of the behaviors and explanations presented in the lessons.

Economics is an exciting and intriguing social science. My goal in developing this course is to empower you to make intelligent decisions that increase economic well-being by understanding economic relationships.

—Ranita Wyatt

Course Organization

Choices and Change: Macroeconomics is designed as a comprehensive learning package consisting of four elements: student course guide, textbook, video programs, and interactive activities (optional).

STUDENT COURSE GUIDE

The guide for this course is:

>Wyatt, Ranita. *Student Course Guide for Choices & Change: Macroeconomics.* New York: Worth Publishers, 2009. ISBN (10): 1-4292-4008-3; (13): 978-1-4292-4008-6

This student course guide acts as your daily instructor. For each lesson it gives you an Overview, Lesson Assignments, Lesson Objectives, Lesson Focus Points, a Practice Test, and an Answer Key. If you follow the student course guide recommendations and study each lesson carefully, you should successfully meet all of the requirements for this course.

TEXTBOOK

In addition to the student course guide, the textbook required for this course is:

>Krugman, Paul and Robin Wells. *Macroeconomics.* 2nd ed. New York: Worth Publishers, 2009. ISBN (10): 0-7167-7161-6; (13): 978-0-7167-7161-6

VIDEO PROGRAMS

The video program series for this course is:

>*Choices & Change: Macroeconomics.*

Each video program is correlated with the student course guide and the reading assignment for that lesson. Be sure to read the Lesson Focus Points in the student course guide before you watch the program. The video programs are presented in a documentary format and are divided into distinct but connected segments. Every video brings analysis and perspective to the issues being discussed. Watch them closely.

If the video programs are broadcast more than once in your area, or if DVDs, CDs, videotapes, and streaming are available at your college, you might find it helpful to watch the video programs more than once for review. Since examination questions will be taken from the video programs as well as from the reading, careful attention to both is vital to your success.

INTERACTIVE COURSE

Self-graded interactive exercises, pre- and post-self-assessments, and case-based, problem-solving scenarios are available to students whose institutions have opted to offer these. These activities are useful for reinforcement and review of lesson content and learning objectives. The interactive activities are offered in two formats: CD-ROM and Internet. Ask your instructor how to access these activities if they are listed in your syllabus as a course requirement.

Course Guidelines

Follow these guidelines as you study the material presented in each lesson:

1. OVERVIEW:
   Read the Overview for an introduction to the lesson material.

2. LESSON ASSIGNMENTS:
   Review the Lesson Assignments in order to schedule your time appropriately. Pay careful attention, as the titles and numbers of the textbook chapter, the student course guide lesson, and the video program may be different from one another.

3. LESSON OBJECTIVES:
   To get the most from your reading, review the Lesson Objectives in the student course guide; then read the assignment.

4. LESSON FOCUS POINTS
   The Lesson Focus Points are designed to help you get the most benefit from the resources selected for each lesson. To maximize your learning experience:
   a. Scan the focus point questions.
   b. Read the assigned textbook pages.
   c. View the video.
   d. Write answers to the focus point questions. (References in parentheses following each question can be used to locate information in the text and video that relates to each question.)

5. REVIEW
   The following process is intended to help you retain the knowledge you have acquired in this lesson.
   - Review key points in the "Quick Reviews" at the end of each section in the textbook.
   - Complete the "Check Your Understanding" questions at the end of each section and check your answers using the answer key at the end of the textbook.
   - Review the case studies in "Economics in Action" in the textbook.
   - Review the critical concepts noted in the page margins of the textbook.
   - Complete the following Practice Test and check your responses.
   - Revisit the text and/or video for any questions you answer incorrectly on the Practice Test.

6. PRACTICE TEST:
   Complete the Practice Test to help you evaluate your understanding of the lesson.

7. ANSWER KEY:
   Use the Answer Key at the end of the lesson to check your answers or to locate material related to each question of the Practice Test.

8. **LESSON INTERVIEWEES**
   These individuals are being acknowledged for their valuable contributions to this course. The titles and locations were accurate when the video programs were recorded, but may have changed since the original taping.

Lesson 1

The Study of Choice

OVERVIEW

The field of economics exists because resources are limited, but the potential uses for resources are unlimited. Therefore, individuals and societies must make *choices* in the use of these scarce resources. Scarcity forces all societies to answer the basic fundamental questions of what to produce, how to produce, and who consumes what is produced. How these questions are answered is primarily determined by the economic structure of each society.

Resources are used in the production of goods (tangible output) and services (intangible output). Microeconomics deals with decisions or choices that must be made by individuals and businesses. Macroeconomics analyzes choices from the viewpoint of the society as a whole. In a nutshell, economics is a social science that studies how societies and individuals choose to allocate their scarce resources. When choices are made, individuals receive *utility* or satisfaction from consuming goods and services.

One of the most important economic concepts presented in this lesson is that choice involves cost. Opportunity cost represents the value of what is given up when a choice is made. An individual makes thousands of choices every day, as do institutions and government entities. Choices are affected by many variables, and sometimes difficult choices must be made. The video highlights a school district in Los Angeles faced with making some decisions about additional funds. There are a wide variety of needs and potential uses for these funds. The school board president, principals, teachers, businesses, teacher's union, parents, and students all have competing uses for school funds. Opinions vary greatly on what is best for the school as a whole as well as the individual.

The expression "a picture is worth a thousand words" explains why graphs are an essential element for understanding economic theories and concepts. The graphs are developed in the video, step-by-step, in order to simplify complex relationships. You will reap the most benefits throughout the course if extra effort is spent on becoming comfortable with reading and creating graphs.

An assumption that helps economists formulate and make predictions about the economy is "Ceteris Paribus," a Latin phrase that basically means "all other variables held constant." By holding all other factors constant that might affect the relationship between one variable and another, an economist is able to isolate the unique effects of a particular variable.

Normative and positive views are highlighted in the segment featuring the North American Free Trade Agreement (NAFTA) treaty and the different perceptions of its success. Opinions come from all angles and there is seldom complete agreement. There are many "gray areas" in this ongoing discussion.

LESSON ASSIGNMENTS

Text: Krugman and Wells. *Macroeconomics*, Introduction, "The Ordinary Business of Life," pp. 1–4; Chapter 1, "First Principles," pp. 5–22; Chapter 2, "Economic Models: Trade-offs and Trade," pp. 24–25, 37–38; Chapter 2 Appendix, pp. 45–60; Chapter 6, "Macroeconomics: The Big Picture," pp. 154–156

Video: "The Study of Choice" from the series *Choices & Change: Macroeconomics*

LESSON OBJECTIVES

1. Define economics, scarcity, opportunity cost, utility, and the term *ceteris paribus*.

2. Discuss the fundamental economic questions all societies must answer.

3. Distinguish between macroeconomics and microeconomics.

4. Distinguish between normative and positive economic statements.

5. Explain the use of models in the science of economics.

6. Explain the difference between goods and services.

7. Utilize graphical representations of theories and data for analysis.

8. Create a line graph from a table of data.

9. Calculate the slope of a line from a graph.

LESSON FOCUS POINTS

The following questions are designed to help you get the most benefit from the resources selected for this lesson. To maximize your learning experience:

    a. Scan the focus point questions.
    b. Read the assigned text pages.
    c. View the video.
    d. Write answers to the following questions. (References in parentheses can be used to locate information in the text and video that will help you answer the question.)

1. Define the following terms and concepts: economics, scarcity, opportunity cost, and utility. (textbook, pp. 2–7; video segment 2; student course guide Lesson 1 Overview)

2. What is the *ceteris paribus* assumption, and why is it necessary when conducting economic analysis? (textbook, p. 24; student course guide Lesson 1 Overview)

3. List the fundamental economic questions that all societies must answer. (student course guide Lesson 1 Overview)

4. The discipline of economics can be broken down into two areas: macroeconomics and microeconomics. It has been said that in macroeconomics we are studying the forest and in microeconomics we are studying the trees. Do you agree or disagree with this analogy? Briefly explain your answer. (textbook, pp. 154–156; student course guide Lesson 1 Overview; video segment 4)

5. Give an example of a normative statement and a positive statement in the video. Explain the difference. (textbook, pp. 37–38; video segment 4)

6. Models are abstractions or oversimplifications of the real world. Why do economists use models to establish simple basic economic relationships? (textbook, pp. 24–25)

7. What are the characteristics of a good? What are the characteristics of a service? Use examples to illustrate. (student course guide Lesson 1 Overview)

8. Create three graphs. One should represent a positive relationship, one a negative relationship, and one no relationship. Explain each relationship. (textbook, pp. 47–48; video segment 3)

9. Graph the information in the following data set. What are the intercepts? (textbook, pp. 45–48)

Good Z

Price (P)	Quantity Demanded (Q_d)
$ 1	50
2	40
3	30
4	20
5	10

10. Calculate the slope of the line from the data in question 9. (textbook, pp. 48–52)

REVIEW

The following process is intended to help you retain the knowledge you have acquired in this lesson.

- Review key points in the "Quick Reviews" at the end of each section in the textbook.
- Complete the "Check Your Understanding" questions at the end of each section and check your answers using the answer key at the end of the textbook.
- Review the case studies in "Economics in Action" in the textbook.
- Review the critical concepts noted in the page margins of the textbook.
- Complete the following Practice Test and check your responses.
- Revisit the text and/or video for any questions you answer incorrectly on the Practice Test.

PRACTICE TEST

Multiple Choice: Circle the letter that corresponds to the BEST answer for each question.

1. Economics is different from other social sciences because it is primarily concerned with the study of _____; it is similar to other social sciences because they are all concerned with the study of _____.
   A. unlimited resources; economic systems
   B. human interactions; limited resources
   C. social behavior; scarcity
   D. scarcity; human interactions
   E. people; unlimited resources

2. The existence of alternative uses of a resource implies that it is _____.
   A. free
   B. scarce
   C. expensive
   D. plentiful
   E. unlimited in supply

3. The problem of determining what goods and services society should produce exists because _____.
   A. resources are plentiful
   B. resources are scarce
   C. most of our resources are privately rather than socially owned
   D. most of our resources are socially rather than privately owned
   E. other countries can provide us with most of the things that we now produce ourselves

Lesson 1—The Study of Choice

4. An answer to the question "How are goods produced?" determines _____.
   A. who receives the goods that are produced
   B. how tastes and preferences are determined
   C. how resources are combined in the production of goods
   D. the quantity of society's natural resource endowments
   E. the types and quantities of goods and services produced

5. Opportunity cost is _____.
   A. $10 if the first unit is $20
   B. the dollar payment for a product
   C. the benefit derived from a product
   D. the value of the best alternative forgone when the choice is made
   E. the value of the best alternative received when the choice is made

6. One question that arises when determining for whom goods and services should be produced is: _____
   A. "Who pays what share of taxes?"
   B. "Who gets how much of the economic pie?"
   C. "How can we import more goods for domestic consumption?"
   D. "How can we reduce exports so as to leave more goods for domestic consumption?"
   E. "Should taxes be reduced so that people have more income to spend?"

7. The satisfaction people receive from consuming goods and services or engaging in some activities is _____.
   A. marginal
   B. utility
   C. maximization
   D. economics
   E. economy

8. Microeconomics is most likely to be concerned with the _____
   A. economy as a whole.
   B. activity of large segments of the economy.
   C. economic behavior of specific parts or units of the economy.
   D. economywide trends in unemployment, prices, and production.
   E. "forest" of economic behavior, rather than the individual "trees."

9. An example of a normative statement is: _____.
   A. The rate of unemployment is 4 percent
   B. A high rate of economic growth creates more jobs for the country
   C. The federal government spends half of its budget on national defense
   D. Everyone in the country needs to be covered by national health insurance
   E. Baseball players are paid higher salaries than the president of the United States

Lesson 1—The Study of Choice

10. A tangible commodity that people value is _____.
    A. an economy
    B. a good
    C. a market
    D. a service
    E. a margin

11. A simplified representation of a particular problem is a _____.
    A. model
    B. constant
    C. hypothesis
    D. law
    E. variable

12. Macroeconomics is most likely to be concerned with the _____
    A. amount of unemployment in a specific industry.
    B. economic behavior of a particular household.
    C. economic behavior of specific parts or units of the economy.
    D. "forest" of economic behavior, rather than the individual "trees."
    E. "trees" of economic behavior, rather than the entire "forest."

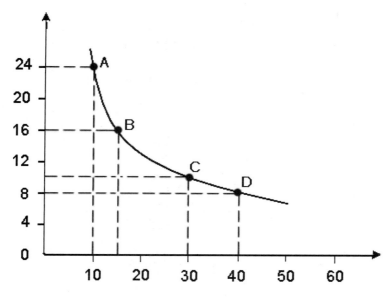

Use the graph above to answer the following three questions.

13. The curve on the graph above illustrates _____.
    A. an inverse relationship between the variables
    B. no relationship between the variables
    C. a direct relationship between the variables
    D. a lateral relationship between the variables
    E. a horizontal relationship between the variables

14. The slope of the line between points A and B equals _____.
    A. +8/5
    B. −5/8
    C. +5/8
    D. −8/5
    E. 0

15. The slope of the line between points C and D equals _____.
    A. +1/5
    B. +5/1
    C. −1/5
    D. −5/1
    E. +1

Lesson 1—The Study of Choice

Short-answer essay questions.

16. Create a graph to illustrate the information in the table below.

Income	Consumption
0	200
100	275
200	350
300	425
400	500
500	575
600	650
700	725
800	800
900	875
1000	950

17. What is a possible explanation for the shape of the curve you have drawn?

18. Provide an example of a normative statement from the Los Angeles School District segment in the video.

19. Provide an example of a positive statement from the Los Angeles School District segment.

ANSWER KEY

1. D ....LO 1 ....Krugman/Wells, p. 2; video segment 2
2. B ....LO 1 ....Krugman/Wells, p. 6; video segment 2
3. B ....LO 1 ....Krugman/Wells, p. 6; video segment 2
4. C ....LO 2 ....Wyatt, student course guide Lesson 1 Overview
5. D ....LO 1 ....Krugman/Wells, p. 7
6. B ....LO 2 ....Wyatt, student course guide Lesson 1 Overview
7. B ....LO 1 ....Wyatt, student course guide Lesson 1 Overview
8. C ....LO 3 ....Krugman/Wells, pp. 154–155; Wyatt, student course guide Lesson 1 Overview
9. D ....LO 4 ....Krugman/Wells, pp. 37–38
10. B ....LO 6 ....Wyatt, student course guide Lesson 1 Overview
11. A ....LO 5 ....Krugman/Wells, pp. 24–25
12. D ....LO 3 ....Krugman/Wells, pp. 154–155; Wyatt, student course guide Lesson 1 Overview
13. A ....LO 7 ....Krugman/Wells, pp. 47–48; video segment 3
14. D ....LO 9 ....Krugman/Wells, pp. 48–51
15. C ....LO 9 ....Krugman/Wells, pp. 48–51

Short-answer essay questions.

16. LO 8..................Krugman/Wells, pp. 45–47

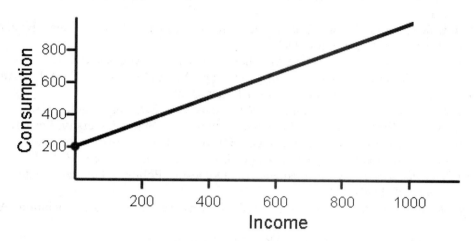

17. LO 7..................Krugman/Wells, pp. 47–48
People tend to increase their spending as their income increases.

18. LO 4..................Krugman/Wells, pp. 37–38; video segments 2 and 4
"The most important thing I think we should spend more money on would be after-school programs."

19. LO 4..................Krugman/Wells, pp. 37–38; video segments 2 and 4
"The largest share of any school district money is going to be in salaries and benefits."

LESSON INTERVIEWEES

Julia Alvarado, Car Buyer, Dallas, TX

Daniel J. Barnhart, Teacher, Downtown Business Magnet High School, LAUSD, Los Angeles, CA

Bret Caldwell, Spokesman, Communications Coordinator, International Brotherhood of Teamsters, Washington, DC

Victoria M. Castro, Trustee, Board Member, LAUSD, Los Angeles, CA

Steve Condly, Teacher, Downtown Business Magnet High School, LAUSD, Los Angeles, CA

Anita Davis, Student, University of North Texas, Denton, TX

Downtown Business Magnet High School Students, LAUSD, Los Angeles, CA

Soumen Ghosh, Environmental Economist, New Mexico State University, Las Cruces, NM

Gus Herring, Professor of Economics, Brookhaven College, Farmers Branch, TX

Day Higuchi, President, United Teachers of Los Angeles, Los Angeles, CA

Merrill Matthews Jr., Vice-President of Domestic Policy, National Center for Policy Analysis, Dallas, TX

Martin Rojas, Director, International Affairs, American Trucking Association, Alexandria, VA

Mike Roos, President and CEO, LEARN, Los Angeles, CA

Ron Sakoda, Principal, Downtown Business Magnet High School, LAUSD, Los Angeles, CA

Judy Scales, Parent, LAUSD, Los Angeles, CA

Paul Truax, Southwest Regional Representative, Reform Party USA, Addison, TX

Manuel Vasquez, Production Assistant, Dallas, TX

Lesson 2

Confronting Scarcity

OVERVIEW

This lesson develops the production possibilities curve (PPC) which is the first economic model in this course. The production possibilities curve (or frontier) is a graphical representation of the possible combinations of output that could be produced. The curve is developed with the assumption that resources and technology are fixed and fully utilized at a given point in time.

It is important to understand that the curve represents production efficiency in the use of available resources and technology. Resources are divided into three categories: land, labor, and capital. Many economists include a fourth category, entrepreneurship, as an important component. Entrepreneurs combine the other factors of production in exchange for potential profit. If the level or quality of resources changes, then the PPC changes. Technological innovations also lead to economic growth or an increase in production possibilities.

One of the most important characteristics of this model is opportunity cost. If all resources and technology are being utilized efficiently, increasing the production of one good results in a *cost*, which is the amount of other goods that cannot be produced. If opportunity cost remains constant, the shape of the PPC will be linear (a straight line) with a constant slope.

In reality, resources are not equally suitable for all types of production; therefore, opportunity cost increases. If production occurs on the PPC, then the cost of producing additional units of a good or service requires giving up larger and larger amounts of the other goods and services. This effect is referred to as the *law of increasing opportunity cost* and is graphically portrayed with a concave or bowed-out PPC (its slope is not constant).

Although the entire production possibilities curve represents production efficiency, only one point on a curve exhibits allocative efficiency. Allocative efficiency occurs when the combination of goods and services society desires the most is produced. This combination cannot be derived directly from the PPC.

The rain forest segment focuses on the many different uses for the land, the trees, and other resources located within the rain forest. However we may not know the true costs of destroying rain forest from clear cutting and mining. For example, we may be destroying potential discoveries of new drugs or other medicinal miracles.

Production possibilities curves shift outward to illustrate economic growth or inward to illustrate economic decline. These shifts are often caused by changes in the quantity or quality of resources.

The PPC can also be utilized to illustrate the potential benefits from international trade. When countries specialize in the production of goods and services where a comparative advantage exists and then trade with each other, they are able to reach consumption combinations outside their own production possibilities.

Decisions about production vary from country to country. Economies fall somewhere between the extremes of command (socialism) and market economy (pure capitalism) in this process. Nearly all economies are a mixture of the two. A market economy has very limited amounts of government involvement; however, capitalism relies on the concept of private property ownership which requires laws and, therefore, government.

The major distinction between a command economy and a market economy is ownership of the resources. In the command system the government owns or controls the resources and decides how the resources are to be used. The government answers the fundamental economic questions of what to produce, how to produce, and who consumes what is produced. In a market system individuals are the ultimate owners of the factors of production (resources) and they also answer the fundamental economic questions.

LESSON ASSIGNMENTS

Text: Krugman and Wells. *Macroeconomics*, Chapter 1, "First Principles," pp. 14–16; Chapter 2, "Economic Models: Trade-offs and Trade," pp. 23–44

Video: "Confronting Scarcity" from the series *Choices & Change: Macroeconomics*

LESSON OBJECTIVES

1. Define factors of production.

2. Explain a production possibilities curve and its assumptions.

3. Explain the law of increasing opportunity cost and how it relates to the production possibilities curve.

4. Use the production possibilities curve to illustrate efficient and inefficient levels of production.

5. Distinguish between allocative efficiency and production efficiency.

6. Explain economic growth and the causes of growth.

7. Utilize a production possibilities curve to illustrate economic growth.

8. Define comparative advantage, specialization, and the law of increasing opportunity cost.

9. Explain how international trade affects the production of trading partners.

10. Discuss the strengths and weaknesses of market capitalism and command socialism.

11. Describe the generally accepted roles for government in a market economy.

LESSON FOCUS POINTS

The following questions are designed to help you get the most benefit from the resources selected for this lesson. To maximize your learning experience:

   a. Scan the focus point questions.
   b. Read the assigned text pages.
   c. View the video.
   d. Write answers to the following questions. (References in parentheses can be used to locate information in the text and video that will help you answer the question.)

1. What are the types of economic resources (factors of production)? (textbook, p. 29)

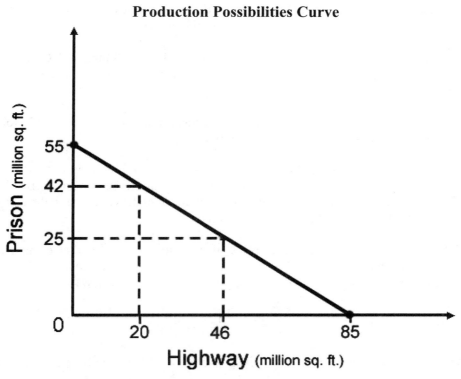

Use the graph above to answer the following three questions.

2. If the state is currently choosing to build 46 million square feet of highway and 25 million square feet of prisons, what is the opportunity cost of increasing prison footage to 42 million square feet? (textbook, pp. 25–28; video segment 2)

3. Using the graph above, illustrate the effect of a technological advancement that requires less concrete to maintain the same amount of strength. (textbook, pp. 28–30; video segment 2)

4. In terms of the graph above, illustrate and explain where efficient and inefficient production occurs. (textbook, pp. 26–27)

5. Graphically illustrate the production possibilities curve for the rain forest example shown in the video. What assumptions did you make when developing the curve? Explain why it should have a concave shape. (textbook, pp. 27–28; video segment 3)

6. Using the rain forest example, explain the difference between production efficiency and allocative efficiency. (textbook, p. 27; student course guide Lesson 2 Overview)

7. Use the rain forest PPC to illustrate economic growth. What are the possible factors to cause this effect? (textbook, pp. 28–30; video segment 3)

8. Illustrate a decline in a country's production possibilities and provide potential causes for the decline. (textbook, pp. 25–30; video segment 3)

9. Create production possibilities curves for the United States and Germany in terms of cameras and computers from information in the video. (textbook, pp. 25–28; video segment 4)

10. Use the PPCs created for question 9 to illustrate and explain the basis for international trade. (textbook, pp. 30–34; video segment 4)

11. The two extremes of economic systems—capitalism and socialism—differ in regard to who owns property resources and how resources are to be allocated. Briefly explain this difference. What are the advantages and disadvantages of capitalism and socialism? (student course guide Lesson 2 Overview)

12. What are the major economic roles of government in a market economy? Why is it necessary for government to play these roles in a market economy? Briefly explain. (textbook, pp. 14–16; student course guide Lesson 2 Overview)

REVIEW

The following process is intended to help you retain the knowledge you have acquired in this lesson.

- Review key points in the "Quick Reviews" at the end of each section in the textbook.
- Complete the "Check Your Understanding" questions at the end of each section and check your answers using the answer key at the end of the textbook.
- Review the case studies in "Economics in Action" in the textbook.
- Review the critical concepts noted in the page margins of the textbook.
- Complete the following Practice Test and check your responses.
- Revisit the text and/or video for any questions you answer incorrectly on the Practice Test.

PRACTICE TEST

Multiple Choice: Circle the letter that corresponds to the BEST answer for each question.

1. The three broad types of resources used to produce goods and services are also known as _____.
    A. economic systems
    B. factors of production
    C. production possibilities
    D. economic efficiency
    E. financial capital

2. Capital is best considered as _____.
    A. the natural environment
    B. produced resources
    C. financial assets
    D. human effort
    E. money

Production Possibilities Schedule

Production Alternatives

	V	W	X	Y	Z
Capital goods	0	1	2	3	4
Consumer goods	20	18	14	8	0

Use the table above to answer the following two questions.

3. If the economy is producing alternative W, the real cost of producing at X is _____ units of consumer goods.
    A. 0
    B. 2
    C. 4
    D. 14
    E. 18

4. The production combination of 8 units of Consumer Goods and 5 units of Capital Goods _____.
    A. is the production point that will give the most satisfaction to this economy
    B. is unattainable given current resources and technology
    C. fully employs all available resources and technology
    D. represents an inefficient use of resources
    E. represents an efficient use of resources

5. If an economy has to sacrifice increasing amounts of good X for each unit of good Y produced, then its production possibilities curve is _____.
   A. a straight line
   B. a vertical line
   C. a horizontal line
   D. bowed out from the origin
   E. bowed in toward the origin

6. If an economy is producing a combination of goods that places it on the production possibilities curve, then it has _____.
   A. inflation
   B. economic growth
   C. full employment
   D. inefficiency
   E. idle factors

7. By specializing in the production of a few goods, a nation is _____.
   A. less likely to make efficient use of available resources
   B. more likely to engage in international trade
   C. able to become self-sufficient
   D. able to ignore the opportunity cost of production
   E. unable to develop a comparative advantage

8. The United States imports some goods and exports other goods primarily because of _____.
   A. free goods
   B. unemployment
   C. self-sufficiency
   D. comparative advantage
   E. the law of decreasing opportunity cost

9. Increases in resources or improvements in technology will tend to cause a society's production possibilities curve to _____.
   A. shift inward to the left
   B. shift outward to the right
   C. remain unchanged
   D. become horizontal
   E. become vertical

10. The economy's factors of production are not equally suitable for producing different types of goods. This principle generates _____.
    A. economic growth
    B. technical efficiency
    C. resource underutilization
    D. the law of increasing cost
    E. full employment of the economy's resources

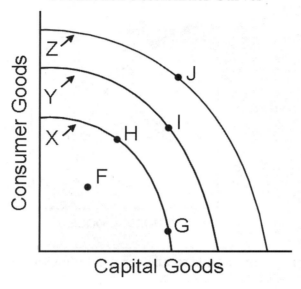

Production Possibilities Curves

Use the graph above to answer the following three questions.

11. Production efficiency is achieved at point _____ with respect to curve _____.
    A. G; Y
    B. I; Y
    C. J; Y
    D. H; Y
    E. F; X

12. Which point illustrates allocative efficiency?
    A. G
    B. H
    C. I
    D. J
    E. Not enough information

13. Which point(s) illustrates inefficiency with respect to curve Y?
    A. J
    B. G
    C. H
    D. I
    E. Points G and H

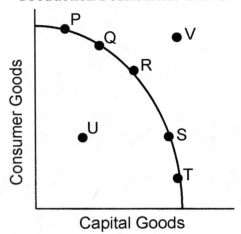

Production Possibilities Curve

Use the graph above to answer the following two questions.

14. Production at Point U indicates that the economy _____.
    A. is producing the maximum output with available resources and technology
    B. has unemployed resources
    C. is efficient in production
    D. is operating inefficiently
    E. both B and D

15. The point representing a combination of consumer goods and capital goods that can be attained only by economic growth is point _____.
    A. Q
    B. U
    C. R
    D. V
    E. T

16. In a market capitalist economy, _____.
    A. there is no government intervention
    B. resources are government owned, but individuals make some decisions over their use
    C. resources are government owned, and government exercises broad power over their use
    D. resources are privately owned, and individuals make decisions over their use
    E. resources are privately owned, but government exercises broad power over their use

17. Government's role of protecting property rights is considered _____.
    A. enforcing a legal system
    B. providing certain goods and services
    C. redistributing income
    D. maintaining the money supply
    E. expanding economic growth

18. Which of the following might contribute to economic growth?
    A. An increase in the average education level of the population
    B. Technological innovation
    C. A decrease in unemployment
    D. All of the above
    E. Both A and B

Short-answer essay questions.

19. What does a production possibilities curve illustrate? List the PPC's assumptions.

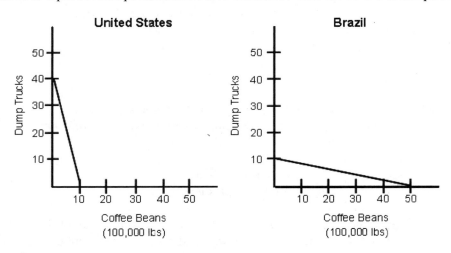

20. Use the PPCs above to draw a graph to illustrate the production possibilities curve if trade existed between the United States and Brazil.

ANSWER KEY

1. B ....LO 1 ....Krugman/Wells, p. 29; video segment 1
2. B ....LO 1 ....Krugman/Wells, p. 29
3. C ....LO 4 ....Krugman/Wells, pp. 27–28; video segment 2
4. B ....LO 4 ....Krugman/Wells, pp. 26–27; video segment 3
5. D ....LO 3 ....Krugman/Wells, pp. 27–28; video segment 3
6. C ....LO 4 ....Krugman/Wells, pp. 26–27; video segment 3
7. B ....LO 9 ....Krugman/Wells, pp. 30–34; video segment 4
8. D ....LO 8 ....Krugman/Wells, pp. 30–33; video segment 4
9. B ....LO 6 ....Krugman/Wells, pp. 28–30; video segment 5
10. D ....LO 3, 8 .....Krugman/Wells, pp. 27–28; video segment 2
11. B ....LO 5 ....Krugman/Wells, p. 27
12. E ....LO 5 ....Krugman/Wells, p. 27; Wyatt, student course guide Lesson 2 overview
13. E ....LO 4 ....Krugman/Wells, pp. 26–27
14. E ....LO 4 ....Krugman/Wells, pp. 26–27
15. D ....LO 7 ....Krugman/Wells, pp. 28–29
16. D ....LO 10 ....Wyatt, student course guide Lesson 2 Overview
17. A ....LO 11 ....Wyatt, student course guide Lesson 2 Overview
18. E ....LO 6 ....Krugman/Wells, pp. 28–30

Short-answer essay questions.

19. LO 2........................Krugman/Wells, pp. 25–27; video segment 2
    A production possibilities curve is developed with the assumptions that
    a. resources are fixed
    b. technology is fixed
    c. resources and technology are used efficiently
    d. only two types of goods are being produced

The PPC illustrates different combinations of the maximum output that can be produced given the level of resources and technology and assuming efficient use of those inputs.

20. LO 9........................Krugman/Wells, pp. 30–34; video segments 4 and 5

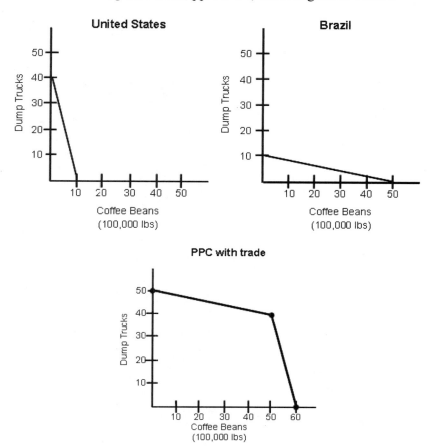

LESSON INTERVIEWEES

Sterling Gordon, Director of Quality Assurance, Coffee Holding Company, Inc., Brooklyn, NY
William C. Gruben, Chief International Economist, Federal Reserve Bank of Dallas, Dallas, TX
Jack Lascar, Vice-President of Investor Relations, Terex Corporation, Westport, CT
Linwood Pendleton, Assistant Professor of Economics, University of Southern California, Los Angeles, CA
Russell Pollero, Owner, Friendly Forest Products, Miami, FL
Libby Rittenberg, Professor of Economics, Colorado College, Colorado Springs, CO

Lesson 3

Supply and Demand

OVERVIEW

This lesson presents one of the most important tools for economic analysis: supply and demand. The textbook presents all the mechanics of the supply and demand curves; however, to assist you in understanding the graphs, the video develops the curves and illustrates how to use the curves for analysis. Equilibrium price and quantity are important concepts for you to understand. Determining the changes in equilibrium due to changes in supply and/or demand is also essential.

The video starts with the step-by-step development of the curves through the graphing of a generic demand curve. Knowing the difference between a *change in demand* (the curve shifts due to a change in a determinant) and a *change in quantity demanded* (a movement along the curve due to a change in price) is essential. After the demand curve development segment, we move into a segment illustrating a consumer's demand for landscaping plants for a small suburban neighborhood backyard. Watch for factors that cause a change in demand for particular kinds of plants.

Next is the step-by-step development of a supply curve. As in the demand curve, knowing the difference between a *change in supply* (the curve shifts due to a change in a determinant) and a *change in quantity supplied* (a movement along the curve due to a change in price) is essential. After the supply curve development, we move back to the landscaping example but from the producer's point of view (supply). Watch for factors that cause a change in supply. Then, the supply and demand curves are utilized to find equilibrium price and quantity. This segment also illustrates shifting the curves and determining the changes in equilibrium as a result of the shifts.

The interviews in the State Fair segment focus on how owners determine prices and quantities offered for sale. Notice that although some of the vendors cannot immediately respond to shortages or surpluses of the good or service they are offering, the Belgian waffle maker can. The livestock segment focuses on the reason people show their animals. Winning translates into an increase in the value of the animal and, therefore, the price received for the livestock in the auction increases.

The last part of this video provides examples of markets that do not achieve equilibrium due to outside forces such as government price controls. Usury laws and limits on interest rates are examples of a price ceiling (legal maximum price) which leads to a shortage of loanable funds. Minimum wage is an example of a price floor (legal minimum price) which many will argue causes surpluses of labor or unemployment. As in most subjects, there is disagreement over the usefulness and desirability of price controls.

Your understanding of and ability to utilize supply and demand curves as tools for economic analysis are essential at this point for success in this course. If you do not have a firm grasp of this material at the end of the lesson, please contact your instructor.

LESSON ASSIGNMENTS

Text: Krugman and Wells. *Macroeconomics*, Chapter 3, "Supply and Demand," pp. 61–92, and Chapter 4, "The Market Strikes Back," pp. 93–106

Video: "Supply and Demand" from the series *Choices & Change*: *Macroeconomics*

LESSON OBJECTIVES

1. Define demand.
2. Explain the difference between a change in demand and a change in quantity demanded.
3. Explain how price affects the demand curve.
4. Create a demand curve from a demand schedule.
5. Explain how the demand shifters (determinants of demand) affect the demand curve.
6. Define supply.
7. Explain the difference between a change in supply and a change in quantity supplied.
8. Explain how price affects the supply curve.
9. Create a supply curve from a supply schedule.
10. Explain how the supply shifters (determinants of supply) affect the supply curve.
11. Use supply and demand curves to find equilibrium price and quantity.
12. Calculate shortages and surpluses that occur when market price does not equal equilibrium price.
13. Explain how shortages and surpluses are eliminated in a market economy.
14. Explain what happens to equilibrium price and quantity when there is a change in supply, demand, or both.
15. Explain the effect of a price floor on a market.
16. Explain the effect of a price ceiling on a market.

LESSON FOCUS POINTS

The following questions are designed to help you get the most benefit from the resources selected for this lesson. To maximize your learning experience:

    a. Scan the focus point questions.
    b. Read the assigned text pages.
    c. View the video.
    d. Write answers to the following questions. (References in parentheses can be used to locate information in the text and video that will help you answer the question.)

1. What is a demand curve? What is the result of a change in price? (textbook, pp. 62–66; video segment 2)

2. List the determinants (demand shifters) of demand and explain how they affect the demand curve. (textbook, pp. 66–70; video segment 2)

3. The following list of prices and corresponding quantities demanded (Q_D) is referred to as a demand schedule. Graph the demand schedule, placing price on the vertical axis and quantity demanded on the horizontal axis. (textbook, pp. 63–64; video segment 2)

Price	Q_D
$10.00	20
11.00	18
12.00	16
13.00	14
14.00	12
15.00	10

4. Illustrate the difference between a change in demand and a change in quantity demanded on the demand curve from the previous question. (textbook, pp. 64–66; video segment 2)

5. What is a supply curve? What is the result of a change in price? (textbook, pp. 71–74; video segment 3)

6. List the determinants (supply shifters) of supply and explain how they affect the supply curve. (textbook, pp. 72–77; video segment 3)

7. The following list of prices and corresponding quantities supplied (Q_S) is referred to as a supply schedule. Graph the supply schedule, placing price on the Y-axis (vertical) and quantity supplied on the X-axis (horizontal). (textbook, pp. 71–72; video segment 3)

Price	Q_S
$10.00	10
11.00	13
12.00	16
13.00	19
14.00	21
15.00	24

8. Illustrate the difference between a change in supply and a change in quantity supplied on the supply curve from the previous question. (textbook, pp. 72–74; video segment 3)

9. Include the demand curve you created from question #3 and the supply curve you created from question #7 on the same graph. Equilibrium occurs at the intersection of supply and demand or where quantity supplied and quantity demanded are equal. Highlight this point on your graph. What is the equilibrium price and quantity? (textbook, pp. 78–80; video segment 4)

10. Utilize the supply and demand curves from question #9 to calculate the effect if the market price is $14. Is there a shortage or a surplus? How much? If price is $11, what is the resulting shortage or surplus? (textbook, pp. 80–82; video segment 4)

11. At any price above equilibrium, the result will be a surplus. Explain the process a freely operating market will experience to eliminate a surplus. Include changes in quantities demanded and supplied. (textbook, p. 80; video segment 4)

12. At any price below equilibrium, the result will be a shortage. Explain the process a freely operating market will experience to eliminate a shortage. Include changes in quantities demanded and supplied. (textbook, pp. 81–82; video segment 4)

13. Draw graphs to demonstrate each of the following: (textbook, pp. 83–87)
    A. an increase in demand; illustrate what happens to equilibrium price and quantity.
    B. a decrease in demand; illustrate what happens to equilibrium price and quantity.
    C. an increase in supply; illustrate what happens to equilibrium price and quantity.
    D. a decrease in supply; illustrate what happens to equilibrium price and quantity.
    E. an increase in both supply and demand; illustrate what happens to equilibrium price and quantity.
    F. an increase in supply and a decrease in demand; illustrate what happens to equilibrium price and quantity.
    G. a decrease in both supply and demand; illustrate what happens to equilibrium price and quantity.
    H. an increase in demand and a decrease in supply; illustrate what happens to equilibrium price and quantity.

14. Briefly explain the result of government-imposed prices as contrasted with prices determined by supply and demand. (textbook, pp 94–105; video segment 5)

15. Define a price floor. Would the price floor be set above or below equilibrium to have an affect on the market? What is an example of a price floor and what is its result? (textbook, pp. 101–105; video segment 5)

16. Define a price ceiling. Would the price ceiling be set above or below equilibrium to have an affect on the market? What is an example of a price ceiling and what is its result? (textbook, pp. 94–99)

REVIEW

The following process is intended to help you retain the knowledge you have acquired in this lesson.

- Review key points in the "Quick Reviews" at the end of each section in the textbook.
- Complete the "Check Your Understanding" questions at the end of each section and check your answers using the answer key at the end of the textbook.
- Review the case studies in "Economics in Action" in the textbook.
- Review the critical concepts noted in the page margins of the textbook.
- Complete the following Practice Test and check your responses.
- Revisit the text and/or video for any questions you answer incorrectly on the Practice Test.

PRACTICE TEST

Multiple Choice: Circle the letter that corresponds to the BEST answer for each question.

1. The relationship between the price of a good, the quantity people are willing and able to purchase, and the independent variables that determine quantity is _____.
   A. supply
   B. demand
   C. equilibrium
   D. disequilibrium
   E. production possibilities

2. Consumer preferences, prices of other goods, income, and demographic characteristics are often termed _____.
   A. market technologies
   B. demand prices
   C. demand shifters
   D. supply determinants
   E. supply quantities

Movie Tickets

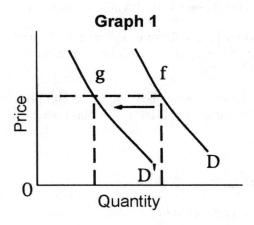

Graph 1

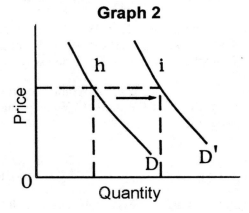

Graph 2

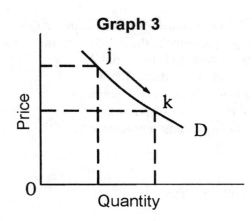

Graph 3

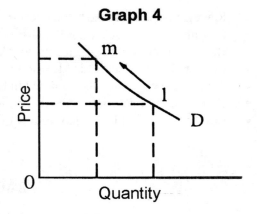

Graph 4

Use the graphs above to answer the following two questions.

3. An increase in the fee charged for movie tickets would result in a change illustrated by _____.
   A. the move from f to g in Graph 1
   B. the move from h to i in Graph 2
   C. the move from j to k in Graph 3
   D. the move from l to m in Graph 4
   E. none of the graphs presented above

4. An increase in the price of popcorn would result in a change illustrated by _____.
   A. the move from f to g in Graph 1
   B. the move from h to i in Graph 2
   C. the move from j to k in Graph 3
   D. the move from l to m in Graph 4
   E. none of the graphs presented above

5. Given that meat and potatoes are complementary goods, if the price of meat decreases substantially, _____.
   A. the demand for potatoes increases
   B. the quantity of potatoes demanded increases
   C. the demand for potatoes decreases
   D. the quantity of potatoes demanded decreases
   E. the demand for potatoes does not change

6. Economists know that a particular good can be classified as an inferior good if _____ in buyers' income causes _____.
   A. an increase; an increase in demand
   B. an increase; an increase in quantity demanded
   C. an increase; a decrease in demand
   D. an increase; a decrease in quantity demanded
   E. a decrease; a decrease in demand

7. If the price of a commodity increases, you expect the _____.
   A. demand to decrease
   B. quantity demanded to increase
   C. quantity demanded to decrease
   D. demand curve to shift to the right
   E. demand curve to shift to the left

8. Supply is best defined as the _____.
   A. amount of a commodity that sellers would be willing and able to sell at a specific price
   B. price that buyers would be willing and able to pay for a specific quantity of a good
   C. Relationship between the price of a good and the quantity people want to purchase of a good
   D. relationship between the price of a good and the quantity people want to sell of a good
   E. relationship between the quantity of a good people want to purchase and the quantity of a good people want to sell

9. If the price of a commodity increases, you expect the _____.
   A. supply to increase
   B. quantity supplied to increase
   C. quantity supplied to decrease
   D. supply curve to shift to the right
   E. supply curve to shift to the left

Movie Tickets

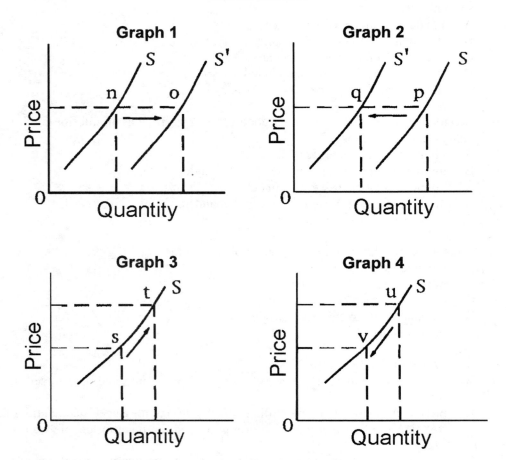

Use the graphs above to answer the following two questions.

10. An increase in the number of movie theaters would result in a change illustrated by _____.

    A. the move from n to o in Graph 1
    B. the move from p to q in Graph 2
    C. the move from s to t in Graph 3
    D. the move from u to v in Graph 4
    E. none of the graphs presented above

11. An increase in the ticket price would result in a change illustrated by _____.

    A. the move from n to o in Graph 1
    B. the move from p to q in Graph 2
    C. the move from s to t in Graph 3
    D. the move from u to v in Graph 4
    E. none of the graphs presented above

12. An example of a supply shifter is _____.
    A. demographic characteristics
    B. a burst of new technology
    C. income
    D. consumer expectations
    E. consumer preferences

13. A decrease in supply is caused by _____.
    A. a decrease in resource prices
    B. an increase in the number of sellers in the market
    C. suppliers' expectations of higher prices in the future
    D. an advancement in the technology for producing the good
    E. a decrease in the price of a good using the same resources

14. If the quantity of available housing in a community is greater than the quantity of houses demanded, the existing price _____.
    A. remains unchanged
    B. rises to clear the market
    C. either rises or remains unchanged
    D. is below the market equilibrium price
    E. is above the market equilibrium price

15. In a competitive market, if there is a shortage of a product at a given price, _____.
    A. sellers drive the price down
    B. sellers drive the price up
    C. buyers drive the price down
    D. buyers drive the price up
    E. the price tends to remain constant

16. In a competitive market, if there is a surplus of a product at a given price, _____.
    A. sellers drive the price down
    B. sellers drive the price up
    C. buyers drive the price down
    D. buyers drive the price up
    E. the price tends to remain constant

17. An increase in demand and a decrease in supply leads to _____ in equilibrium quantity and _____ in equilibrium price.
    A. a decrease; a decrease
    B. an indeterminate change; an increase
    C. an indeterminate change; a decrease
    D. an increase; an indeterminate change
    E. a decrease; an indeterminate change

Supply and Demand Schedules for a Good

Price (per unit)	Quantity Demanded (units)	Quantity Supplied (units)
$2.00	350	200
2.50	290	220
3.00	240	240
3.50	200	250
4.00	160	260
4.50	130	270
5.00	100	280

Use the table above to answer the following four questions.

18. The equilibrium price is _____ and the equilibrium quantity is _____.
    A. $2.00; 230 units
    B. $3.00; 240 units
    C. $4.00; 210 units
    D. more than $5.00; less than 100 units
    E. impossible to determine; impossible to determine

19. An effective price floor could be set at a price of _____ and would cause a _____.
    A. $4.50; a shortage of 140 units
    B. $2.00; a surplus of 150 units
    C. $2.50; a shortage of 70 units
    D. $5.00; a surplus of 180 units
    E. $3.50; a surplus of 40 units

20. If demand increased 50 units, the new equilibrium price and quantity would be _____ and _____ units, respectively.
    A. $2.00; 310
    B. $2.50; 295
    C. $3.00; 290
    D. $3.50; 250
    E. more than $3.50; more than 250

21. An effective price ceiling could be set at a price of _____ and would cause a _____.
    A. $4.50; a surplus of 140 units
    B. $2.00; a shortage of 110 units
    C. $2.50; a shortage of 70 units
    D. $5.00; a surplus of 180 units
    E. $3.50; a shortage of 50 units

Lesson 3—Supply and Demand

22. A decrease in demand and a decrease in supply leads to _____ in equilibrium quantity and _____ in equilibrium price.
    A. a decrease; a decrease
    B. an indeterminate change; an increase
    C. an indeterminate change; a decrease
    D. an increase; an indeterminate change
    E. a decrease; an indeterminate change

23. Which of the following would cause a decrease in the current demand for cars?
    A. A decrease in income if cars are a normal good
    B. Consumers expect the price of cars to decrease in the future
    C. A decrease in the number of car dealerships
    D. All of the above
    E. Both A and B

24. If cold weather in Boston decreases consumer preferences for ice cream while at the same time there is a decrease in the price of the ingredients used to make ice cream, what will happen to the equilibrium price and quantity of ice cream?
    A. Equilibrium quantity will increase and equilibrium price will decrease
    B. Equilibrium quantity will decrease and equilibrium price will increase
    C. Equilibrium price will decrease, but the change in equilibrium quantity is indeterminate
    D. Equilibrium quantity will decrease, but the change in equilibrium price is indeterminate
    E. Both equilibrium price and quantity will decrease

25. If producers of mp3 players expect the market price of mp3 players to decrease in the future, the current supply of mp3 players will _____, leading to a(n) _____ in the equilibrium price and a(n) _____ in the equilibrium quantity.
    A. decrease; decrease; increase
    B. increase; decrease; increase
    C. increase; increase; increase
    D. decrease; increase; decrease
    E. increase; increase; decrease

Short-answer essay questions.

Supply and Demand Schedules for a Good

Price (per unit)	Quantity Demanded (units)	Price (per unit)	Quantity Supplied (units)
$2.00	350	2.00	200
2.50	290	2.50	220
3.00	240	3.00	240
3.50	200	3.50	250
4.00	160	4.00	260
4.50	130	4.50	270
5.00	100	5.00	280

Use the table above to answer the following five questions.

26. Use the information in the table above to graph a demand curve.

27. Use the information in the table above to graph a supply curve.

28. Combine the supply and demand curves from the previous two questions. What is the equilibrium price and quantity?

29. Graphically illustrate the effect of an increase in the price of inputs on equilibrium price and quantity.

30. Graphically illustrate the effect of an increase in demand on equilibrium price and quantity.

ANSWER KEY

1. B .... LO 1 .... Krugman/Wells, pp. 62–64; video segment 2
2. C .... LO 5 .... Krugman/Wells, pp. 66–70; video segment 2
3. D .... LO 2, 3 .... Krugman/Wells, pp. 62–66; video segment 2
4. A .... LO 2, 5 .... Krugman/Wells, pp. 66–70; video segment 2
5. A .... LO 2, 5 .... Krugman/Wells, pp. 67–68
6. C .... LO 2, 5 .... Krugman/Wells, p. 68
7. C .... LO 3 .... Krugman/Wells, pp. 64–66; video segment 2
8. D .... LO 6 .... Krugman/Wells, pp. 71–72
9. B .... LO 8 .... Krugman/Wells, pp. 72–74; video segment 3
10. A .... LO 7, 10 .... Krugman/Wells, pp. 72–77
11. C .... LO 7, 8 .... Krugman/Wells, pp. 71–74; video segment 3
12. B .... LO 10 .... Krugman/Wells, pp. 74–77; video segment 3
13. C .... LO 10 .... Krugman/Wells, pp. 74–77
14. E .... LO 12, 13 .... Krugman/Wells, pp. 80–81; video segment 4
15. D .... LO 13 .... Krugman/Wells, pp. 81–82; video segment 4
16. A .... LO 13 .... Krugman/Wells, p. 80; video segment 4
17. B .... LO 14 .... Krugman/Wells, pp. 85–87
18. B .... LO 11 .... Krugman/Wells, pp. 78–80; video segment 4
19. D .... LO 15 .... Krugman/Wells, pp. 80–82, 101–102
20. D .... LO 11, 14 .... Krugman/Wells, pp. 78–80
21. C .... LO 16 .... Krugman/Wells, pp. 80–82, 94–96
22. E .... LO 14 .... Krugman/Wells, pp. 85–87
23. E .... LO 5 .... Krugman/Wells, pp. 66–70
24. C .... LO 5, 10, 14 ..... Krugman/Wells, pp. 68, 75, 83–87
25. B .... LO 10, 14 .... Krugman/Wells, pp. 75–76, 84–85

Short-answer essay questions.

26. LO 4 .... Krugman/Wells, pp. 62–64; video segment 2

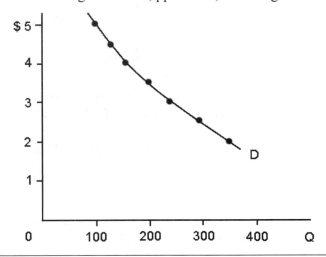

Lesson 3—Supply and Demand

27. LO 9 .... Krugman/Wells, pp. 71–72; video segment 3

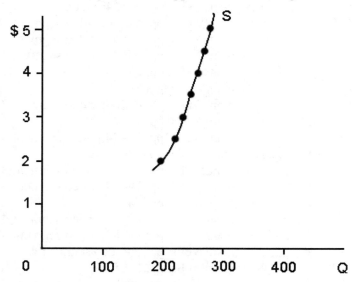

28. LO 11 .... Krugman/Wells, pp. 78–80; video segment 4

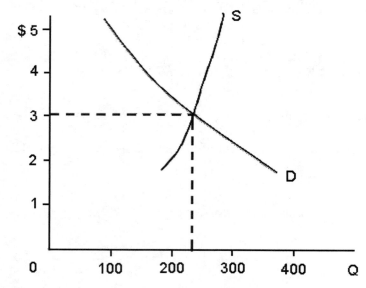

Equilibrium price is $3.00, and equilibrium quantity is 240 units.

29. LO 10, 14...................... Krugman/Wells, pp. 75, 84–85; video segment 4

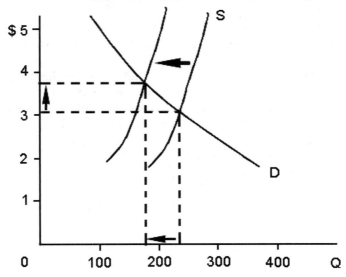

An increase in the price of inputs will cause the supply curve to shift to the left. Equilibrium price will rise and equilibrium quantity will fall.

30. LO 14............................ Krugman/Wells, pp. 83–85; video segment 4

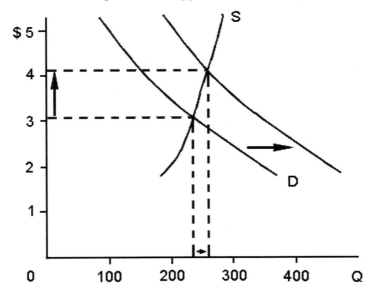

An increase in demand will shift the demand curve to the right. Equilibrium price and quantity will both increase.

Lesson 3—Supply and Demand

LESSON INTERVIEWEES

Billy Baxter, Owner, Space Roller, State Fair of Texas, Dallas, TX

Jeffery T. Collins, Ph.D., Economist, University of Arkansas, Center on Business and Economics, Fayetteville, AR

Diana Furchtgott-Roth, Resident Fellow, American Enterprise Institute, Washington, DC

Theresa Ghilarducci, Professor of Economics, University of Notre Dame, Notre Dame, IN

Howard Hamilton, Executive Vice-President, McIlroy Bank & Trust Co., Fayetteville, AR

Jack D. Hildinger Jr., Sales Representative, McHutchenson Horticulture and Distributors, Double Oak, TX

Lisa Hildinger, Homemaker, Double Oak, TX

Dennis Poole, Borden County 4H, Gail, TX

Tanner Poole, Borden County 4H, Gail, TX

Norman Zable, President, N.Z. Properties Inc., Dallas, TX

Lesson 4

The Business Cycle

OVERVIEW

This lesson focuses on the phases of the business cycle. The business cycle is characterized by alternating periods of expansion and contraction of economic activity. When the economy contracts, gross domestic product (GDP) and the dollar value of an economy's output declines and unemployment rises. When the economy expands, GDP increases and unemployment decreases. If the expansion approaches or exceeds normal capacity, then inflation is often the consequence. It is important to understand that due to capacity and technological limitations, the economy cannot expand indefinitely. The government often tries to moderate the business cycles in an attempt to avoid the consequences of the extreme fluctuations.

Unemployment is divided into four categories: frictional, seasonal, cyclical, and structural. Unemployment increases during the contraction phase of the business cycle and is called *cyclical unemployment*, which means employment opportunities decrease. When an economy is expanding, more jobs are available and cyclical unemployment declines; however, there still will be some unemployment in the labor force such as frictional and structural unemployment. Frictional unemployment often occurs by choice; for example, quitting a job to find more desirable employment or being a new entrant in the labor market. Frictional unemployment usually lasts for a short period of time. Structural unemployment is due to a mismatch of skills and job locations. This type is usually caused by technological change. Seasonal unemployment occurs when the time of year changes the supply of or demand for labor. For example, the labor force increases in the summertime when students are out of school. Also, there are increases in the demand for labor during the holidays.

If you don't have a job, are you "officially" unemployed? Maybe. Not having a paying job is not the only requirement for being unemployed. In the "real world," there are other requirements that must be met in order to be considered officially unemployed; for example, you must be at least 16 years old, you must not be employed, and *you must be seeking employment*.

The next phases after contraction are recovery and then expansion, which sometimes lead to an inflationary problem. One segment of the video focuses on calculating inflation with price indices and analyzing the causes of inflation. A "real" value is a value in terms of base year prices and a "nominal" value is the value in current prices. A "real" value is found by taking a "nominal" value and dividing by a price index and then multiplying by 100. Economists often do not agree on the accuracy of inflation statistics. The lesson includes the controversy over the accuracy of such measures.

"Time Well Spent" is an article from the 1997 annual report of the Federal Reserve Bank of Dallas. The authors of the article look at the changes in the price of goods and services from the perspective of work time. In other words, how many minutes or hours do you have to work in order to buy a particular good or service? Nearly all prices (in terms of work time) have actually decreased over the last century, with few exceptions.

LESSON ASSIGNMENTS

Text: Krugman and Wells. *Macroeconomics*, Chapter 6, "Macroeconomics: The Big Picture," pp. 153–171; Chapter 7, "Tracking the Macroeconomy," pp. 187–192; Chapter 8, "Unemployment and Inflation," pp. 200–223

Video: "The Business Cycle" from the series *Choices & Change: Macroeconomics*

LESSON OBJECTIVES

1. Describe the phases of the business cycle.
2. Explain the concept of a price index and how it functions.
3. Calculate the rate of inflation or deflation.
4. Interpret CPI figures for different years as to changes in cost of living.
5. Explain the limitations of price indices as measures of well-being.
6. Explain why some people gain and some lose purchasing power due to inflation.
7. Identify the types of unemployment.
8. Identify the criteria that determine unemployment and full employment.
9. Calculate the unemployment rate.
10. Describe the limitations of unemployment statistics.

LESSON FOCUS POINTS

The following questions are designed to help you get the most benefit from the resources selected for this lesson. To maximize your learning experience:

    a. Scan the focus point questions.
    b. Read the assigned text pages.
    c. View the video.
    d. Write answers to the following questions. (References in parentheses can be used to locate information in the text and video that will help you answer the question.)

1. Graphically illustrate the phases of the business cycle. Briefly explain some causes of business cycles. (textbook, pp. 158–161; video segment 2)

2. What is a price index? What is the index in the base year? If the current year's index equals 138, how much has the price level increased since the base year period? (textbook, pp. 187–190; video segment 4)

3. If the CPI for 1992 is 1.424 and the CPI for 1993 is 1.463, what is the inflation rate for 1993? (textbook, pp. 188–189; video segment 4)

4. What factors influence the accuracy of inflation rates calculated with price indices? (textbook, p. 191; video segment 4)

5. If the rate of inflation is calculated to be 3.6 percent, does that mean that well-being has decreased the same percentage? Briefly explain. (video segment 4)

6. Inflation arbitrarily redistributes wealth and income. Explain how the following could be affected by an unanticipated increase in the inflation rate: savers, debtors, fixed income earners, and creditors. What would happen to a worker's real income if the rate of inflation were greater than the nominal wage increase? (textbook, pp. 214–218; video segments 4 and 5)

7. Define the following: frictional unemployment, structural unemployment, and cyclical unemployment. Which type of unemployment is the most undesirable and why? Could some unemployment be desirable in terms of bringing about a more efficient allocation of labor resources? Briefly explain. (textbook, pp. 207–211; student course guide Lesson 4 Overview)

8. Describe the types of unemployment illustrated by the interviewees in the video, "The Business Cycle." (video segment 3)

9. How do you determine whether a person is part of the labor force? What are the requirements for someone to be considered unemployed? Define the natural rate of unemployment. How is the natural rate of employment determined? (textbook, pp. 200–201, 206–207, 210–211; student course guide Lesson 4 Overview; video segment 3)

10. The unemployment rate is the percentage of the labor force that is unemployed. If the labor force is 100,000 and the number of employed is 96,200, what is the unemployment rate? (textbook, pp. 200–201; video segment 3)

11. The Bureau of Labor Statistics (BLS) conducts a monthly survey of approximately 65,000 households to estimate the size of the labor force and the number of unemployed people. What are some potential problems in the BLS's method of estimating the unemployment rate? (textbook, pp. 200–203; video segment 3)

Excerpted with permission from the Federal Reserve Bank of Dallas 1997 Annual Report, "Time Well Spent."

When a product first comes onto the market, it's typically very expensive, affordable for only society's wealthiest. Soon thereafter, though, its price falls quickly and the product spreads throughout society. Once the good or service becomes commonplace, its price usually continues to fall, but at a slower rate. This tendency shows up in such everyday purchases as housing, food, clothing, gasoline, electricity and long-distance telephone service. It also applies to manufactured goods—automobiles, home appliances and the modern age's myriad electronic marvels. And year after year it takes less of our work time to buy entertainment and services—movies, haircuts, airline tickets, dry cleaning and the like. In a very real sense, the cost of living in America keeps getting cheaper. By harnessing the natural power of income distribution, free markets have routinely brought the great mass of Americans products once beyond even the reach of kings.[3]

EXHIBIT 1: *The High Cost of Living, 1897 Style*

Item	1897 Sears catalog price	1997 work-equivalent price*
1 lb. box of baking soda	$ .06	$ 5.34
100 lb. 16d nails	1.70	151.39
Garden hoe	.28	24.94
26" carpenter's saw	.50	44.53
13" nail hammer	.42	37.40
9" steel scissors	.75	66.79
Aluminum bread pan	.37	32.95
Ironing board	.60	53.43
Telephone	13.50	1,202.23
Men's cowboy boots	3.50	311.69
Pair men's socks	.13	11.58
Pair ladies' hose	.25	22.26
200 yd. spool of cotton thread	.02	1.78
Webster's dictionary	.70	62.34
One dozen pencils	.14	12.47
250 manila envelopes	.35	31.17
1 carat diamond ring	74.00	6,590.00
Upright piano	125.00	11,131.76
Bicycle	24.95	2,221.90
Baby carriage	10.25	912.80

* Prices are in terms of how much a manufacturing employee would earn today working the same number of hours required to afford the product in 1897. For example, a 1-pound box of baking soda sold for 6¢ in 1897. At an average hourly wage of 14.8¢ the typical manufacturing worker would have had to labor 24 minutes to earn enough to buy the box of soda. Today, 24 minutes earns that worker $5.34.

Use the table above to answer the following question.

12. The table on the previous page is a partial reprint of an Annual Report by the Federal Reserve Bank of Dallas (1997). Choose five of the items listed and find their current price in current dollars. Calculate the percentage difference between the current dollar price and the work equivalent price. For example:

If the current price of a 1-pound box of baking soda is $1.29, then the percentage change is equal to

$$\frac{1.29 - 5.34}{5.34} = -.76 = -76\%.$$ The current price is 76% less than the equivalent work price.

Based on your calculations, what conclusions can you draw about price changes over the last hundred years? (video segment 5)

REVIEW

The following process is intended to help you retain the knowledge you have acquired in this lesson.

- Review key points in the "Quick Reviews" at the end of each section in the textbook.
- Complete the "Check Your Understanding" questions at the end of each section and check your answers using the answer key at the end of the textbook.
- Review the case studies in "Economics in Action" in the textbook.
- Review the critical concepts noted in the page margins of the textbook.
- Complete the following Practice Test and check your responses.
- Revisit the text and/or video for any questions you answer incorrectly on the Practice Test.

PRACTICE TEST

Multiple Choice: Circle the letter that corresponds to the BEST answer for each question.

1. The sequence of business cycle phases is _____.
   A. peak, trough, expansion, recession
   B. peak, expansion, trough, recession
   C. peak, recession, trough, expansion
   D. peak, expansion, recession, trough
   E. trough, peak, recession, expansion

2. A period of at least two consecutive quarters of falling real GDP is _____.
   A. a peak
   B. a trough
   C. a cycle
   D. an expansion
   E. a recession

3. The point on a business cycle when real GDP stops rising and begins falling is _____.
   A. a peak
   B. a trough
   C. a cycle
   D. an expansion
   E. a recession

4. The expression "too much money chasing too few goods" best describes the condition called _____.
   A. depreciation
   B. expectations
   C. deflation
   D. inflation
   E. fluctuations

5. A number whose movement reflects movement in the average level of prices is _____.
   A. unemployment
   B. inflation
   C. a price index
   D. an unemployment rate
   E. a business cycle

6. The consumer price index reflects the _____.
   A. changes in the prices of goods and services typically purchased by consumers
   B. level of prices for intermediate goods and services purchased by business
   C. level of prices for raw materials
   D. prices of all goods and services computed from the ratio of nominal GDP to real GDP
   E. prices of all goods and services computed from the ratio of nominal GDP to current GDP

7. If the CPI is 120 in Year One and 150 in Year Two, then the rate of inflation from Year One to Year Two is ____ percent.
   A. 10
   B. 20
   C. 25
   D. 50
   E. 150

The Consumer Price Index	
Year	Consumer Price Index
1	80
2 (base)	100
3	105
4	125
5	150

Use the table above to answer the following two questions.

8. The approximate rate of inflation in Year 2 is ____ percent.
   A. 5
   B. 10
   C. 19
   D. 20
   E. 25

9. The approximate value of the dollar in Year 4, relative to the base year, is _____.
   A. $0.67
   B. $0.80
   C. $0.95
   D. $1.00
   E. $1.25

10. If the general price level declines while your money income remains constant, then your real income _____.
    A. fluctuates
    B. increases
    C. decreases
    D. remains constant
    E. will equal your money income

11. If, in a given period, the rate of inflation turns out to be higher than lenders and borrowers anticipated, then the effect will be _____.
    A. a redistribution of wealth from borrowers to lenders
    B. a redistribution of wealth from lenders to borrowers
    C. no change in the distribution of wealth between lenders and borrowers
    D. a net gain in purchasing power for lenders relative to borrowers
    E. a net loss in purchasing power for borrowers relative to lenders

12. An auto assembly-line worker who is laid off when his job function is automated using new technology is _____.
    A. structurally unemployed
    B. cyclically unemployed
    C. frictionally unemployed
    D. underemployed
    E. seasonally unemployed

13. An example of frictional unemployment is _____.
    A. an autoworker who is temporarily laid off from an automobile company due to a decline in sales
    B. a geologist who is permanently laid off from an oil company due to a new technological advance
    C. a worker at a fast-food restaurant who quits work and attends college
    D. a real estate agent who leaves a job in Texas and searches for a similar, higher paying job in California
    E. a corporate executive who decides to retire and permanently leave the labor force

14. Unemployment that occurs when the actual unemployment rate is greater than the natural rate of unemployment is _____.
    A. structural unemployment
    B. cyclical unemployment
    C. frictional unemployment
    D. phantom unemployment
    E. seasonal unemployment

15. The labor force is all _____.
    A. people
    B. people under the age of 64
    C. people working
    D. people unemployed
    E. people working plus the unemployed

16. The natural level of employment occurs if there is no _____.
    A. unemployment
    B. frictional unemployment
    C. transitional unemployment
    D. structural employment
    E. cyclical unemployment

Labor Market Data
(in millions)

	Year 1	Year 2	Year 3	Year 4
Population	100	100	100	100
Working age population	80	75	75	90
Number of employed, 16 years of age and over	60	70	50	70
Number not working, 16 years of age and over	10	5	15	10
Number of unemployed, 16 years of age and over who are actively seeking work	6	3	5	4

Use the table above to answer the following three questions.

17. In Year 1, the size of the labor force is _____ million.
    A. 100
    B. 76
    C. 70
    D. 66
    E. 60

18. In Year 3, the official unemployment rate is _____ percent.
    A. 50
    B. 30
    C. 27.3
    D. 10
    E. 9.1

19. In Year 4, the official unemployment rate is _____ percent.
    A. 5.4
    B. 5.7
    C. 13.5
    D. 14.3
    E. 30

Short-answer essay questions.

20. Graphically illustrate and label a business cycle.

21. According to the video "The Business Cycle," why is the CPI an inaccurate measure for changes in the cost of living?

22. What problems exist in terms of accurately measuring unemployment?

ANSWER KEY

1. C .... LO 1 .... Krugman/Wells, pp. 158–159; video segment 2
2. E .... LO 1 .... Krugman/Wells, p. 160; video segment 2
3. A .... LO 1 .... Krugman/Wells, pp. 158–159; video segment 2
4. D .... LO 1 .... Krugman/Wells, pp. 165–166, 214–215; video segment 4
5. C .... LO 2 .... Krugman/Wells, pp. 187–189; video segment 4
6. A .... LO 2 .... Krugman/Wells, p. 189; video segment 4
7. C .... LO 3 .... Krugman/Wells, p. 189; video segment 4
8. E .... LO 3 .... Krugman/Wells, p. 189; video segment 4
9. B .... LO 4 .... Wyatt, student course guide Lesson 4 Overview; video segment 4
10. B .... LO 4 .... Wyatt, student course guide Lesson 4 Overview; video segment 4
11. B .... LO 6 .... Krugman/Wells, pp. 217–218; video segments 4 and 5
12. A .... LO 7 .... Krugman/Wells, pp. 207–211
13. D .... LO 7 .... Krugman/Wells, pp. 207–208
14. B .... LO 7 .... Krugman/Wells, pp. 207–211
15. E .... LO 8 .... Krugman/Wells, pp. 200–201; video segment 3
16. E .... LO 8 .... Krugman/Wells, pp. 210–211
17. D .... LO 8, 9 .... Krugman/Wells, pp. 200–201; video segment 3
18. E .... LO 8, 9 .... Krugman/Wells, p. 201; video segment 3
19. A .... LO 8, 9 .... Krugman/Wells, p. 201; video segment 3

Short-answer essay questions.

20. LO 1......................Krugman/Wells, pp. 158–159; video segment 2

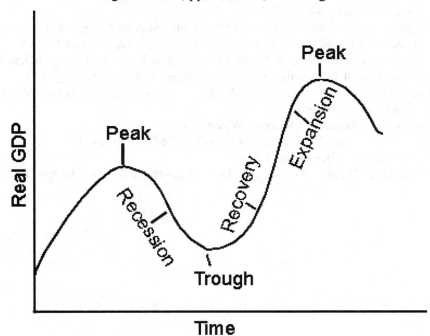

21. LO 5........................Krugman/Wells, pp. 189–191; video segment 4
Since the CPI is a fixed market basket of goods and services, it does not account for substitutions, for example, cucumbers instead of tomatoes. The index also does not account for changes in quality.

22. LO 10......................Krugman/Wells, pp. 201–203; video segment 3
Underemployment and discouraged workers are the main problems in accurately measuring unemployment. Overemployment can also distort figures.

Lesson 4—The Business Cycle

LESSON INTERVIEWEES

Frank Ackerman, Research Assistant Professor, Department of Urban and Environmental Policy, Tufts University, Medford, MA
Patty Harvey, Program Coordinator, Texas Workforce Commission, Arlington, TX
Stephen Moore, Director of Fiscal Policy Studies, The Cato Institute, Washington, DC
Barbara Ridley, Manager Client Services, North Texas Human Resource Group, Allen, TX
Libby Rittenberg, Professor of Economics, Colorado College, Colorado Springs, CO
Jennifer Roberts, Planning and Research Manager, North Central Texas Workforce Development Board, Arlington, TX
Wes Taylor, Network Administrator, Q4i.com, Wylie, TX
Meredith M. Walker, Economist, Federal Reserve Bank of Dallas, Dallas, TX
Deborah Warren, Job Seeker, Greenville, TX
Lloyd A. Webb, Executive Director, North Texas Human Resource Group, Denton, TX

Lesson 5

Measuring Economic Growth

OVERVIEW

This lesson begins with the circular flow model, which is a graphical representation of a private, closed economy without government or international sectors. (The international and government sectors will be added in other lessons.) This model will be revisited throughout the course. The circular flow model illustrates the "symbiotic" or mutually beneficial relationship between consumers and producers. (Throughout this course, the terms *businesses*, *producers*, and *firms* are used interchangeably.) In the simplified version of the model shown in the video, households are the owners of the factors of production (land, labor, capital, and entrepreneurial abilities); therefore, households *supply* these resources to an *input* market. Businesses *demand* these factors of production in order to produce a good or service; then, businesses *supply* the goods and services to the *output* market. In turn, households *demand* the goods and services from the *output* market. These actions represent one of the "flows" in the circular flow model. The other flow is dollars. Households supply resources in exchange for rent, wages, interest, and profit. These dollars are used to pay for the goods and services households demand in the output market. The flow continues as businesses use the sales dollars to pay for the resources used in production.

Segment 2 includes a graphic of the circular flow model. Keep this graphic representation in mind as you watch the video segment about Branson, a small town in Missouri that depends primarily on tourism. This town is used to illustrate the flow of resources and output that make up one of the flows in the model and the dollar flow that makes it all work.

The next segment pertains to measuring economic activity represented by the circular flow model in the economy. The usual measure is gross domestic product (GDP), a term that is familiar to most of us. You will learn about the components used to calculate the value of output or production. You will also learn about some of the difficulties encountered in obtaining accurate measurements. Segment 4 uses the expenditures approach to calculate the value of GDP. The goal is to estimate the dollar value of output (production) in the United States. In this approach, spending on goods and services by consumers, governments, and foreigners (exports) is added to investment spending by businesses. Domestic spending on imports is then subtracted. This sum represents GDP. It is important to note that government spending that is only a transfer of dollars (social security, welfare, unemployment, etc.) is NOT included. Other purely financial transactions, such as stock purchases or monetary gifts, are also not included. Spending on used items is not included since they were counted as part of GDP when the goods were produced.

Note that *investment* refers to *gross* investment instead of *net* investment. Net investment is gross investment minus depreciation. Recall that gross investment is business spending on capital (plant and equipment) plus changes in inventories. Some of the investment in capital is to replace worn out or depreciated plant and equipment; therefore, net investment is a better indicator of potential economic growth. If net investment is negative then the economy has not produced enough capital to replace what was used up, and therefore, the resource base will decline.

Of the four components of GDP (C + I + G + Net Exports) investment is the most volatile. Businesses can change investment plans rather quickly as the economic situation dictates.

Another important measure of economic activity is Net Domestic Product or NDP, which is GDP minus depreciation. Depreciation is sometimes referred to as "capital consumption allowance" since depreciation refers to the reduction in capital from using capital in the production process.

Segment 5 illustrates some of the problems associated with calculating a true dollar value of production. Illegal activities, barter activities, and the value of do-it-yourself activities are just some of the productive activities that are not reflected in GDP statistics. Services produced and purchased in the cleanup of pollution problems are counted as part of output. However, their inclusion in GDP tends to distort the measure of how well a society is actually doing.

The last segment illustrates the use of GDP statistics for comparing the standard of living levels in different countries. Per capita GDP is a better measure for comparing the standards in different countries, yet this is not a perfect measure since there are many intangible factors which have value that cannot be measured or quantified.

LESSON ASSIGNMENTS

Text: Krugman and Wells. *Macroeconomics*, Chapter 2, "Economic Models: Trade-offs and Trade," pp. 35–37; Chapter 7, "Tracking the Macroeconomy," pp. 173–187

Video: "Measuring Economic Growth" from the series *Choices & Change: Macroeconomics*

LESSON OBJECTIVES

1. Draw a simple circular flow model.

2. Interpret a circular flow diagram by explaining the meaning of each of the flow arrows.

3. Explain why the value of final output equals the value of income generated in its production.

4. Define investment (I).

5. Distinguish between GDP and GNP.

6. Calculate the value of GDP using the expenditure approach.

7. Distinguish between real GDP and nominal GDP, GDP and NDP, and net I (investment) and gross I.

8. Explain why taxes and transfer payments are not included in GDP.

9. Identify and explain the conceptual problems associated with estimating GDP.

10. Evaluate the effectiveness of GDP estimates as a measure of economic well-being of an economy.

11. Evaluate the effectiveness of GDP and related measures as a means of comparing different economies.

LESSON FOCUS POINTS

The following questions are designed to help you get the most benefit from the resources selected for this lesson. To maximize your learning experience:

    a. Scan the focus point questions.
    b. Read the assigned text pages.
    c. View the video.
    d. Write answers to the following questions. (References in parentheses can be used to locate information in the text and video that will help you answer the question.)

1. Use the information from the video "Measuring Economic Growth" to create a simple circular flow model of the Branson economy. (textbook, pp. 35–37; video segment 2)

2. Explain the meaning of each of the flow arrows in the circular flow model constructed in the previous question. (textbook, pp. 35–37; video segment 2)

3. Explain the process that leads to income being equal to output or production in an economy. (textbook, pp. 174–178; video segment 2)

4. In economic terms, what is investment? How do inventories relate to investment? (textbook, pp. 174–177 ; video segment 4)

5. Define gross domestic product (GDP) and gross national product (GNP). How do these measures of output differ? (textbook, pp. 177–178, 182)

6. Explain the expenditures approach to calculating GDP. (textbook, pp. 177–180; video segment 4)

Economic Data
(in billions of dollars)

Consumption	5,698.6	Gross investment	1,547.4
Government purchases	1,480.3	Exports	815.2
Imports	1,000.3	Depreciation	650.4

7. Use the information in the table above to calculate the following values:
   A. GDP (textbook, pp. 178–181; video segment 4)
   B. NDP (student course guide Lesson 5 Overview)
   C. Net investment (student course guide Lesson 5 Overview)

8. What are the implications of positive net investment versus negative net investment in regard to economic growth? (student course guide Lesson 5 Overview)

9. What is the difference between real and nominal GDP? When are real and nominal GDP equal? (textbook, pp. 184–185)

10. Why are the following transactions excluded from calculating GDP: financial sales transactions, used goods sales, public and private transfer payments? Why would taxes paid to governments also be excluded from GDP? (textbook, p. 180)

11. GDP may understate the total market value of goods and services produced in a year's time because of nonmarket production and the underground economy. Estimate the value of your productive, nonmarket activities that you do on a weekly basis. (textbook, p. 179; video segment 5)

12. GDP may not be an accurate measure of economic or social well-being. Leisure time, improved product quality, distribution, and pollution are variables that need to be taken into account when assessing our social or economic well-being. Briefly explain how these variables complicate the assessment of GDP as a measure of social or economic well-being. (video segment 5)

13. Since GDP is a measure of economic performance, it may be useful to compare the real GDP of nations. However, comparing real GDP of nations may not provide insight to a country's standard of living. For example, India has a much larger GDP than Switzerland; however, Switzerland has a much higher standard of living. What would be a better measure of a nation's standard of living than real GDP? Briefly explain. (textbook, pp. 185–186; video segment 6)

REVIEW

The following process is intended to help you retain the knowledge you have acquired in this lesson.

- Review key points in the "Quick Reviews" at the end of each section in the textbook.
- Complete the "Check Your Understanding" questions at the end of each section and check your answers using the answer key at the end of the textbook.
- Review the case studies in "Economics in Action" in the textbook.
- Review the critical concepts noted in the page margins of the textbook.
- Complete the following Practice Test and check your responses.
- Revisit the text and/or video for any questions you answer incorrectly on the Practice Test.

PRACTICE TEST

Multiple Choice: Circle the letter that corresponds to the BEST answer for each question.

1. The equality between expenditures on final output and income received from final output implies that GDP is _____.
   A. greater than factor income
   B. equal to factor income
   C. less than factor income
   D. equal to personal consumption expenditures
   E. equal to gross private domestic investment

2. The value of capital goods and services purchased by a business during a given time period is measured by _____.
   A. consumption
   B. investment
   C. government purchases
   D. transfer payments
   E. net exports

3. One reason that investment plays a crucial role in the macroeconomy is that it _____.
   A. is the largest expenditure on GDP
   B. is the smallest expenditure on GDP
   C. represents all purchases by the government sector
   D. represents net purchases by the foreign sector
   E. is very volatile

4. According to the circular flow model, gross domestic income is _____.
   A. greater than gross domestic product
   B. less than gross domestic product
   C. equal to gross domestic product
   D. equal to indirect business taxes
   E. equal to capital consumption allowance

5. In the simple circular flow model, _____.
   A. households supply resources and supply goods and services
   B. businesses demand resources and demand goods and services
   C. households supply resources and demand goods and services
   D. businesses supply resources and supply goods and services
   E. both B and C

Measuring GDP—Expenditure Viewpoint
(in billions of dollars)

Personal consumption	$500
Gross private domestic investment	50
Net exports	−5
State and local government purchases of goods and services	200
Federal government purchases of goods and services	100
Imports	15
Depreciation	45

Use the table above to answer the following three questions.

6. GDP is _____.
   A. $800 billion
   B. $860 billion
   C. $845 billion
   D. $1,000 billion
   E. $1,010 billion

7. NDP is _____.
   A. $800 billion
   B. $860 billion
   C. $845 billion
   D. $1,000 billion
   E. $1,010 billion

8. Net investment is _____.
   A. 95 billion
   B. 50 billion
   C. 45 billion
   D. 5 billion
   E. −5 billion

9. Economic data that reflect actual prices as they existed each year are said to be expressed in terms of _____.
   A. real dollars
   B. nominal dollars
   C. fixed dollars
   D. variable dollars
   E. historical dollars

10. A measure of the economy's output in constant dollars is _____.
    A. intermediate GDP
    B. current GDP
    C. nominal GDP
    D. real GDP
    E. inflation

11. Payments that do not require the recipients to produce a good or service in exchange are _____.
    A. investments
    B. transfer payments
    C. government purchases
    D. consumption
    E. net exports

12. GDP includes _____ expenditures but does not include _____ expenditures.
    A. education; national defense
    B. Social Security; education
    C. Social Security; national defense
    D. national defense; transfer payments
    E. national defense; education

13. One "conceptual problem" of measuring real GDP involves _____.
    A. the service sector
    B. revisions of data
    C. household production
    D. new goods
    E. quality changes

14. One "conceptual problem" of measuring real GDP involves _____
    A. the service sector.
    B. ignoring economic "bads."
    C. revisions of data.
    D. new goods.
    E. quality changes.

Lesson 5—Measuring Economic Growth

Short-answer essay questions.

15. Draw a simple circular flow model. Include arrows to indicate flows and label all parts.

16. What is the difference between GDP and GNP?

17. In terms of the components of GDP, explain why taxes and transfer payments are not part of GDP.

18. Using examples from the video "Measuring Economic Growth," evaluate the usefulness of GDP estimates in relation to economic well-being.

19. In the video "Measuring Economic Growth," what countries are compared in terms of per capita GDP? What is the advantage of using per capita GDP to compare them? Evaluate GDP as a measure of economic well-being as it relates to these examples.

ANSWER KEY

1. B .... LO 3 .... Krugman/Wells, pp. 179–181; video segment 2
2. B .... LO 4 .... Krugman/Wells, p. 177; video segment 4
3. E .... LO 4 .... Wyatt, student course guide Lesson 5 Overview
4. C .... LO 2 .... Krugman/Wells, pp. 174–177
5. C .... LO 1, 2 .... Krugman/Wells, pp. 35–37; video segment 2;
   .... Wyatt, student course guide Lesson 5 Overview
6. C .... LO 6 .... Krugman/Wells, pp. 179–180; video segment 4
7. A .... LO 7 .... Wyatt, student course guide Lesson 5 Overview
8. D .... LO 7 .... Wyatt, student course guide Lesson 5 Overview
9. B .... LO 7 .... Krugman/Wells, pp. 184–185
10. D .... LO 7 .... Krugman/Wells, pp. 184–185
11. B .... LO 8 .... Krugman/Wells, p. 176
12. D .... LO 6, 8 .... Krugman/Wells, p. 180;
    .... Wyatt, student course guide Lesson 5 Overview
13. C .... LO 9 .... Krugman/Wells, p. 179; video segment 5
14. B .... LO 9 .... video segment 5

Short-answer essay questions.

15. LO 1, 2..................Krugman/Wells, p. 35–37; video segment 2

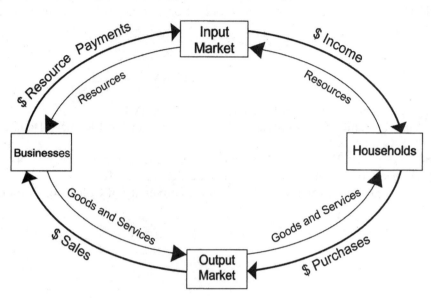

16. LO 5......................Krugman/Wells, p. 182
GDP is the total value of final goods and services produced in the United States in a given time period.
GNP is the total value of final goods and services produced by U.S.-owned resources here and abroad.

17. LO 8......................Krugman/Wells, p. 176
Taxes and transfer payments are dollars changing hands without the recipient exchanging or producing goods or services; therefore, they do not represent production of output.

18. LO 10....................Krugman/Wells, pp. 185–186; video segment 5
One problem in using GDP estimates as a measure of well-being is the value of production that takes place outside of a market. These activities have value but are not counted. Some activities are counted, such as pollution cleanup efforts, but we may not be better off from this increase in GDP.

19. LO 11....................Krugman/Wells, pp. 185–186; video segment 6
The Inuit people of Nunawat are an example of a society with a very low GDP; however, this does not correlate to their quality of life as it does not include the value of maintaining their cultural traditions, social relationships, and social standings. Sweden is an example of a country having a high rate of per capita GDP. Sweden has achieved this with a market capitalist economic policy paired with extensive welfare programs, and there are efforts to ensure that there is not too large of an income disparity among Swedish citizens. India, with a very large population, has a much lower level of per capita GDP and a much larger disparity in income between the rich and the poor.

However, India's per capita GDP does not include the value of household production, which is generally much more extensive and important in developing countries. Using GDP and per capita GDP estimates as measures of well-being have their problems. They do not illustrate the distribution of output or income and are unable to quantify aesthetic values.

LESSON INTERVIEWEES

Corrine Cox, Dancer, Jim Stafford Theater, Branson, MO
Evan Koenig, Senior Economist and Vice-President, Federal Reserve Bank of Dallas, Dallas, TX
Ester Mirjam-Sent, Economist, University of Notre Dame, Notre Dame, IN
Ann Stafford, Co-Owner, Jim Stafford Theater, Branson, MO
Timothy Tregarthen, Professor of Economics, University of Colorado, Colorado Springs, CO

Lesson 6

Aggregate Supply and Demand

OVERVIEW

This lesson introduces the aggregate supply (AS) and aggregate demand (AD) model, which is a simplified representation of an entire economy. This AS/AD model is useful for predicting the effects on inflation and unemployment from changes in the macroeconomy.

The aggregate demand curve represents the demand for all goods and services by all the sectors of the economy at different price levels. The AD curve is downward sloping because of the following:

- Higher price levels translate into higher interest rates; therefore, spending that depends on interest rates decreases. (Some consumer spending and most business spending, i.e., investment, depend on interest rates.)
- Higher domestic price levels lead to increased imports and decreased exports.
- Higher price levels reduce the value of income; therefore, less output can be purchased.

The short-run aggregate supply curve (SRAS) is upward sloping and represents the amount of output businesses will produce at different price levels. Costs of production tend to be fixed in the short run; therefore, higher price levels are incentives to increase production.

The intersection of the AD (aggregate demand) and SRAS curves identifies the amount of output, or GDP, and the corresponding price level where the economy achieves equilibrium. If the economy is not producing that level of output, market pressures will push the economy toward its point of equilibrium. If the economy is producing a larger quantity of output than equilibrium, inventories will rise due to lack of sales, businesses will cut back on production, and the price level will fall in the model. This will continue until there is no longer a buildup of inventories and the economy achieves equilibrium. If output falls short of equilibrium, inventories will decrease. Businesses then increase production and, again, this continues until there is no pressure to increase production.

Not every equilibrium is a desirable equilibrium. The goal is to achieve *full employment* equilibrium where AD (aggregate demand) and SRAS (short-run aggregate supply) intersect at the full employment level of output. This model illustrates full employment output with a long-run aggregate supply (LRAS) curve, which is a vertical line at full employment or potential GDP.

The third segment illustrates the creation of an inflationary gap due to large increases in government spending on the Vietnam War and President Johnson's War on Poverty. An inflationary gap occurs if equilibrium exceeds full employment output, that is, when the SRAS and AD curves intersect to the right of LRAS.

The next segment continues the use of the AS/AD model with an example of a recessionary gap. Graphically this occurs when equilibrium is less than full employment, that is, when the SRAS and AD curves intersect to the left of LRAS. In this segment, the demand for domestic automobiles decreases and the demand for foreign automobiles increases, causing a decrease in AD, which creates a recessionary gap. These changes in AD combined with an oil embargo caused a major decrease in SRAS and led to an unusual case of unemployment in conjunction with inflation. *Stagflation* is the term representing the simultaneous condition of high unemployment and high inflation. This example also highlights the government's involvement in the private sector to save the Chrysler Corporation.

The last segment focuses on the potential for government to manipulate an economy. The government can use fiscal policy (government spending and taxing) or monetary policy (money and credit controls) to influence the economy. When government officials take action for the purpose of changing economic conditions, it is usually called *stabilization policy*. There are many different opinions as to the role of government involvement in our economy, including economists who disagree on this subject.

LESSON ASSIGNMENTS

Text: Krugman and Wells. *Macroeconomics*, Chapter 12, "Aggregate Demand and Aggregate Supply," pp. 315–349

Video: "Aggregate Supply and Demand" from the series *Choices & Change: Macroeconomics*

LESSON OBJECTIVES

1. Define aggregate demand, short-run aggregate supply, full rate of employment, potential level of GDP, sticky wages, equilibrium price level, equilibrium real GDP, recessionary gap, and inflationary gap.

2. Distinguish between movements along an aggregate curve (supply or demand) and shifts in the curve.

3. Explain why aggregate demand has a negative slope.

4. Predict the impact on equilibrium real GDP and price levels of changes in factors that shift aggregate supply.

5. Predict the impact on equilibrium real GDP and price levels of changes in factors that shift aggregate demand.

6. Explain the concept of "sticky" prices and how they affect equilibrium.

7. Describe and graph a recessionary gap.

8. Describe and graph an inflationary gap.

9. Utilize an AS/AD graph to explain the concept of stagflation.

10. Describe and graph how full employment equilibrium may be achieved.

11. Explain the difference between monetary policy and fiscal policy.

12. Explain expansionary policies.

13. Explain contractionary polices.

14. Explain the difference between nonintervention policy and stabilization policy.

LESSON FOCUS POINTS

The following questions are designed to help you get the most benefit from the resources selected for this lesson. To maximize your learning experience:

    a. Scan the focus point questions.
    b. Read the assigned text pages.
    c. View the video.
    d. Write answers to the following questions. (References in parentheses can be used to locate information in the text and video that will help you answer the question.)

1. Define the following terms and concepts: aggregate demand, short-run aggregate supply, full rate of employment, potential level of GDP, long-run aggregate supply, sticky wages, equilibrium price level, equilibrium real GDP, recessionary gap, and inflationary gap. (textbook, pp. 316–341; video segments 2, 3, and 4)

2. Will a change in the price level bring about a change in aggregate supply or aggregate demand? Briefly explain. What will cause a movement from one point along a particular aggregate supply or aggregate demand curve to another point? Briefly explain. (textbook, pp. 320–321 and pp. 326–327; video segment 2)

3. Explain the wealth effect and the interest rate effect in terms of an aggregate demand curve. (textbook, pp. 317–318)

4. What are the determinants of aggregate supply that cause a shift of the aggregate supply curve? In the video "Aggregate Supply and Demand," what causes the aggregate supply curve to shift? Graphically illustrate the effect on equilibrium price levels and equilibrium output levels. (textbook, pp. 327–329 and pp. 336–338; video segment 2)

5. What are the determinants of aggregate demand that cause a shift of the aggregate demand curve? In the video "Aggregate Supply and Demand," what causes the aggregate demand curve to shift? Graphically illustrate the effect on equilibrium price levels and equilibrium output levels. (textbook, pp. 320–323 and pp. 335–336; video segment 2)

6. What is meant by the term *sticky prices*? When there is an increase in aggregate demand in the economy, the price level can increase; however, when there is a decrease in aggregate demand, the overall price level may not decrease. Briefly explain why the overall price level can go up easier than it can go down. (textbook, pp. 324–326)

7. Draw a graph showing the macroeconomy experiencing a recessionary gap. What is happening in a recessionary gap? (textbook, pp. 338–340; video segment 4)

8. Draw a graph showing the macroeconomy experiencing an inflationary gap. What is happening in an inflationary gap? (textbook, pp. 340–341; video segment 3)

9. What will a decrease in aggregate supply do to the overall price level and output levels in the economy? What term do economists use to explain a situation where high inflation and high unemployment occur simultaneously? Utilize an AS/AD graph to illustrate this effect. In the video "Aggregate Supply and Demand," what causes this period of high inflation and unemployment? (textbook, pp. 336–338; student course guide Lesson 6 Overview; video segments 3 and 4)

10. Utilize an AS/AD graph to illustrate and explain how an economy can achieve full employment output, without government interference, if the economy is currently experiencing a recessionary gap. (textbook, pp. 338–340; video segment 2)

11. Monetary and fiscal policies are stabilization tools. How are the two alike and how are they different? (textbook, pp. 320–323; video segment 5)

12. Explain why expansionary policies may be used. Provide an example of an expansionary fiscal and monetary policy. (textbook, pp. 343–344; video segment 5)

13. Explain why contractionary policies may be used. Provide an example of a contractionary fiscal and monetary policy. (textbook, pp. 343–344; video segment 5)

14. Explain nonintervention policy and describe how it differs from stabilization policy. (textbook, pp. 343–345; video segments 5 and 6)

15. The video "Aggregate Supply and Demand" highlights different views from average citizens as well as economists on the subject of government interference in the macroeconomy. In your opinion, what role should the government play in the economy? (video segments 5 and 6)

REVIEW

The following process is intended to help you retain the knowledge you have acquired in this lesson.

- Review key points in the "Quick Reviews" at the end of each section in the textbook.
- Complete the "Check Your Understanding" questions at the end of each section and check your answers using the answer key at the end of the textbook.
- Review the case studies in "Economics in Action" in the textbook.
- Review the critical concepts noted in the page margins of the textbook.
- Complete the following Practice Test and check your responses.
- Revisit the text and/or video for any questions you answer incorrectly on the Practice Test.

PRACTICE TEST

Multiple Choice: Circle the letter that corresponds to the BEST answer for each question.

1. Aggregate demand is the total value of real aggregate GDP that _____.
   A. all sectors of the economy are willing to purchase at various price levels
   B. all sectors of the economy are willing to purchase at various national income levels
   C. consumers are willing to purchase at various price levels
   D. consumers are willing to purchase at various national income levels
   E. all sectors of the economy are willing to sell at various price levels

2. The relationship between the total output produced and the price level, all other things unchanged, is _____.
   A. market supply
   B. surplus supply
   C. national supply
   D. excess supply
   E. aggregate supply

3. The economy's potential real output corresponds to the level of _____.
   A. full employment
   B. frictional unemployment
   C. structural unemployment
   D. natural price level
   E. average prices

4. A recessionary gap occurs if _____.
   A. actual real GDP is less than the potential level of real GDP
   B. actual real GDP is greater than the potential level of real GDP
   C. actual real GDP is equal to the potential level of real GDP
   D. unemployment is less than the natural rate
   E. unemployment is equal to the natural rate

5. The short run in macroeconomic analysis is a period _____.
   A. in which real wages are flexible
   B. in which real wages are sticky
   C. of less than one year
   D. lasting between one and two years
   E. lasting between two and five years

6. When the economy is producing GDP above the potential level, it has _____.
   A. a full-employment GDP
   B. a natural level of employment
   C. a recessionary gap
   D. an inflationary gap
   E. a long-run equilibrium condition

7. An increase in aggregate demand is seen as _____.
   A. a curvature of the aggregate demand curve
   B. a downward movement along the aggregate demand curve
   C. an upward movement along the aggregate demand curve
   D. a shift to the left of the aggregate demand curve
   E. a shift to the right of the aggregate demand curve

8. A movement along the short-run aggregate supply curve in response to a change in the price level is called a _____.
   A. determinant of aggregate supply
   B. revealed cost on aggregate supply
   C. rearrangement of economic production
   D. change in aggregate supply
   E. change in the aggregate quantity of goods and services supplied

9. The downward-sloping aggregate demand curve suggests that _____.
   A. people will buy more goods at higher prices than at lower prices
   B. the public's real cash balances are larger at higher price levels than at lower price levels
   C. the public's real cash balances are negative when the price level is rising
   D. foreigners will buy more exported goods at higher domestic price levels
   E. people will import more foreign goods at higher domestic price levels

10. The decrease in the purchasing power of consumer and business money holdings that occurs when there is an increase in the aggregate price level is known as the _____.
    A. wealth effect
    B. international trade effect
    C. fiscal policy effect
    D. interest rate effect
    E. recessionary effect

11. If the government raises taxes, the aggregate demand curve will _____ and the short-run level of real GDP will _____.
    A. shift to the right; decrease
    B. shift to the left; decrease
    C. shift to the right; increase
    D. shift to the left; increase
    E. not change; decrease

12. If an increase in the average educational attainment of the population leads to increased worker productivity, _____ and the price level will _____.
    A. aggregate demand will increase; increase
    B. aggregate supply will increase; decrease
    C. aggregate supply will decrease; increase
    D. the aggregate quantity of goods and services supplied will increase; decrease
    E. the aggregate quantity of goods and services demanded will decrease; increase

13. A decrease in aggregate supply will generate _____ in short-run real GDP and _____ in the price level.
    A. an increase; an increase
    B. an increase; a decrease
    C. a decrease; an increase
    D. a decrease; a decrease
    E. no change; no change

14. An increase in investment leads to _____ in the price level and _____ in real GDP.
    A. an increase; no change
    B. a decrease; no change
    C. no change; no change
    D. an increase; an increase
    E. a decrease; a decrease

15. An inflationary gap occurs if _____.
    A. actual real GDP is less than potential real GDP
    B. actual real GDP is greater than potential real GDP
    C. actual real GDP is equal to potential real GDP
    D. unemployment is greater than the natural rate
    E. unemployment is equal to the natural rate

16. When the economy is producing GDP below the potential level, it has _____.
    A. a full-employment output
    B. a natural level of employment
    C. a recessionary gap
    D. an inflationary gap
    E. an equilibrium condition

17. A recessionary gap is automatically closed by _____ wages that shift the _____.
    A. lower; SRAS curve to the right
    B. lower; LRAS curve to the right
    C. lower; SRAS curve to the left
    D. higher; SRAS curve to the right
    E. higher; SRAS curve to the left

18. A policy of intervention, aimed at shifting the aggregate demand curve in an effort to close a recessionary or an inflationary gap, is _____.
    A. a welfare policy
    B. a noninterventionist policy
    C. an intermediate policy
    D. a stabilization policy
    E. an advanced policy

19. A policy that allows the economy to close a recessionary or an inflationary gap through self-correction is _____.
    A. a welfare policy
    B. a noninterventionist policy
    C. an intermediate policy
    D. a stabilization policy
    E. an advanced policy

20. A decrease in aggregate demand will generate _____ in short-run real GDP and _____ in the price level.
    A. an increase; no change
    B. a decrease; no change
    C. a decrease; a decrease
    D. no change; an increase
    E. no change; a decrease

21. A decrease in raw materials costs leads to _____ in the price level and _____ in real GDP.
    A. an increase; a decrease
    B. a decrease; an increase
    C. an increase; no change
    D. a decrease; no change
    E. no change; no change

Shifts of the AD/SRAS Curves

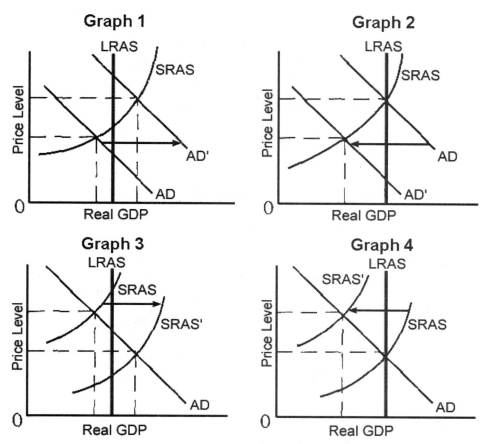

Use the graphs above to answer the following three questions.

22. Which graph(s) depicts the creation of a recessionary gap?
    A. Graph 1
    B. Graph 2
    C. Graph 3
    D. All of the above
    E. None of the above

23. Which graph(s) depicts the creation of an inflationary gap?
    A. Graph 1
    B. Graph 2
    C. Graph 3
    D. Graph 4
    E. Graphs 1 and 3

24. Which graph depicts the creation of stagflation?
    A. Graph 1
    B. Graph 2
    C. Graph 3
    D. Graph 4
    E. None of the above

Short-answer essay questions.

25. Explain how "sticky" wages and prices may prevent markets or an economy from achieving equilibrium.

26. In the video "Aggregate Supply and Demand," what is an example of fiscal policy? How does fiscal policy differ from monetary policy?

27. What is expansionary policy?

28. What is contractionary policy?

ANSWER KEY

1. A ..... LO 1 .... Krugman/Wells, pp. 316–317; video segment 2
2. E ..... LO 1 .... Krugman/Wells, p. 324; video segment 2
3. A ..... LO 1 .... Krugman/Wells, pp. 329–331; video segment 2
4. A ..... LO 1,7 ..... Krugman/Wells, pp. 338–340; video segment 4
5. B ..... LO 1 .... Krugman/Wells, pp. 324–327, 332; video segment 2
6. D ..... LO 1, 8 .... Krugman/Wells, p. 340; video segment 3
7. E ..... LO 2 .... Krugman/Wells, pp. 320–321; video segment 2
8. E ..... LO 2 .... Krugman/Wells, pp. 327–329; video segment 2
9. E ..... LO 3 .... Wyatt, student course guide Lesson 6 overview; segment 2
10. D ..... LO 3 .... Krugman/Wells, pp. 317–318
11. B ..... LO 5 .... Krugman/Wells, pp. 320–323
12. B ..... LO 2, 4 .... Krugman/Wells, pp. 327–329
13. C ..... LO 4 .... Krugman/Wells, pp. 336–337; video segment 2
14. D ..... LO 5 .... Krugman/Wells, pp. 322, 335–336
15. B ..... LO 1, 8 .... Krugman/Wells, p. 340; video segment 3
16. C ..... LO 1, 7 .... Krugman/Wells, pp. 338–340; video segment 4
17. A ..... LO 10 ...... Krugman/Wells, pp. 340–341; video segment 3
18. D ..... LO 14 ...... Krugman/Wells, pp. 343–344; video segment 5
19. B ..... LO 14 ...... Krugman/Wells, p. 343; video segment 6
20. C ..... LO 5 .... Krugman/Wells, pp. 335–336
21. B ..... LO 4 .... Krugman/Wells, pp. 328, 336–337; video segment 2
22. B ..... LO 7 .... Krugman/Wells, pp. 338–340; video segment 4
23. E ..... LO 8 .... Krugman/Wells, pp. 340–341; video segment 3
24. D ..... LO 9 .... Krugman/Wells, pp. 336–337; Wyatt, student course guide Lesson 6 Overview

Short-answer essay questions.

25. LO 6........................Krugman/Wells, pp. 324–327, 331–333
    Since wages are often fixed in the short run due to contracts or other employment agreements and prices tend to change slowly, changes in market demand or market supply will cause shortages or surpluses that may persist. The "stickiness" of wages and prices will keep markets from achieving equilibrium.

26. LO 11......................video segment 5
    In the video "Aggregate Supply and Demand," government spending on programs to reduce poverty and defense spending during the Vietnam War are both examples of fiscal policy. Professor Mason cited the need for a contraction of the money supply and increases in interest rates to slow the inflation of this time period. Altering the money supply and interest rates represents monetary policy.

27. LO 12......................Krugman/Wells, pp. 343–345; video segment 5
    Expansionary policy is aimed at increasing output production and employment, which reduces recessionary problems. Increases in government spending and/or decreases in taxes are expansionary fiscal policy. Increasing the money supply and/or decreasing interest rates is expansionary monetary policy. Expansionary policies cause an increase in the aggregate demand curve.

28. LO 13......................Krugman/Wells, pp. 343–345; video segment 5
    Contractionary policy is aimed at decreasing output production and employment, which reduces inflationary problems. Decreases in government spending and/or increases in taxes are contractionary fiscal policy. Decreasing the money supply and/or increasing interest rates is contractionary monetary policy. Contractionary policies cause a decrease in the aggregate demand curve.

LESSON INTERVIEWEES

Kari L. Battaglia, Lecturer, Department of Economics, University of North Texas, Denton, TX
Teresa Ghilarducci, Economist, University of Notre Dame, Notre Dame, IN
Thomas J. Hern, Chair, Automotive Marketing Department, Northwood University, Cedar Hill, TX
Dr. Magnus L. Kpakol, Business Economist and Adjunct Professor of Economics, University of North Texas and University of Dallas, Denton and Irving, TX
Patrick Mason, Professor of Economics, Florida State University, Tallahassee, FL

Lesson 7

Economic Growth

OVERVIEW

Most societies have a goal of achieving consistent economic growth. Ideally, the economy will grow or expand at a faster rate than the population expands, which usually translates into an increase in the standard of living. Achieving economic growth has many obstacles. In addition to changing economic forces, social and political factors often present major barriers.

Segment 2 examines the factors of growth by highlighting the major economic achievements of Japan since World War II. One area in which Japan has excelled is the formation of capital. Capital formation is very important for an economy to grow; however, this requires sacrifices in terms of goods and services. If resources are used to produce capital or increase the quality of capital, including human capital, then the resources cannot be used to produce goods and services for current consumption. The rate of savings in an economy is also a very important factor; this determines the available funds for investment in capital production. It is important to note that people may or may not be willing to give up current consumption in exchange for potential increases in consumption in the future. Another important influence on economic growth in Japan has been the emphasis on education.

Segment 3 provides a contrast to the economic growth seen in Japan. It focuses on some of the countries of the former Soviet Union and their attempt to achieve growth in a very unstable economic situation. Most of the former Soviet countries are trying to create market-based economies. The video highlights how problems created by ethnic conflicts and the destruction of productive resources interfere with achieving this goal. The Soviet Union experienced massive growth since its creation in the early 1900s; however, the costs were extreme in terms of the sacrifices the population was forced to make in order to achieve these high rates of growth. Millions of people died due to resources being used for capital formation rather than producing food and shelter.

Segment 4 focuses on the problems that developing countries must overcome in order to grow and prosper. Excessive population, inadequate infrastructure, a high level of inequality in income distribution, and agrarian-based economies are some of the problems developing countries must face. These enormous obstacles may require internationally backed assistance to overcome them. The World Bank and the International Monetary Fund (IMF) are two institutions created in 1944 for this purpose. The goals of both institutions are to assist developing countries; however, their methods differ. There is not universal agreement on how to help these countries increase their standard of living.

LESSON ASSIGNMENTS

Text: Krugman and Wells. *Macroeconomics*, Chapter 9, "Long-Run Economic Growth," pp. 225–256, and Chapter 12, "Aggregate Demand and Aggregate Supply," pp. 329–331

Video: "Economic Growth" from the series *Choices & Change: Macroeconomics*

LESSON OBJECTIVES

1. Use an AS/AD graph to illustrate economic growth.

2. List the factors that affect the level of economic growth.

3. Explain the relationship between economic growth and the standard of living.

4. Explain the challenges faced by many developing countries striving for economic growth.

5. Discuss the pros and cons of government aid to developing countries.

6. Explain the challenges related to an economy changing from a command system to a market system.

7. Discuss the relationship between economic growth and the environment.

LESSON FOCUS POINTS

The following questions are designed to help you get the most benefit from the resources selected for this lesson. To maximize your learning experience:

    a. Scan the focus point questions.
    b. Read the assigned text pages.
    c. View the video.
    d. Write answers to the following questions. (References in parentheses can be used to locate information in the text and video that will help you answer the question.)

1. Graphically illustrate the history of Japan since 1944 with AS/AD curves. (video segment 2)

2. Why is economic growth desirable? Based on the video "Economic Growth," list the reasons for Japan's recovery after WWII. (textbook, pp. 225–228; video segment 2)

3. Economic growth implies a shift of the long-run aggregate supply curve to the right. How does economic growth relate to the standard of living? (textbook, pp. 225–228 and pp. 329–331; video segment 1)

4. Based on the video "Economic Growth," explain some of the problems Russia is experiencing in transforming its economic system. (video segment 3)

5. What are the main differences between the World Bank and the International Monetary Fund? (video segment 4)

6. What are the characteristics of low-income countries? What are the challenges faced by developing countries trying to achieve higher standards of living? (textbook, pp. 230–231, 235–236, 238–245; video segment 4)

7. What are some of the criticisms of the World Bank and IMF policies for developing countries? (video segment 4)

8. What is the relationship between real GDP per capita and a country's natural resources? What is sustainable growth? Is economic growth sustainable? Explain the relationship between economic growth and the environment. (textbook, pp. 235–236, 247–252)

REVIEW

The following process is intended to help you retain the knowledge you have acquired in this lesson.

- Review key points in the "Quick Reviews" at the end of each section in the textbook.
- Complete the "Check Your Understanding" questions at the end of each section and check your answers using the answer key at the end of the textbook.
- Review the case studies in "Economics in Action" in the textbook.
- Review the critical concepts noted in the page margins of the textbook.
- Complete the following Practice Test and check your responses.
- Revisit the text and/or video for any questions you answer incorrectly on the Practice Test.

PRACTICE TEST

Multiple Choice: Circle the letter that corresponds to the BEST answer for each question.

1. Economic growth is the _____.
   A. efficiency with which an input is converted to an output
   B. process through which increasingly larger quantities of inputs are needed to produce a given quantity of output
   C. process through which the economy's natural level of real GDP is increased
   D. difference between actual real GDP and potential real GDP
   E. amount of aggregate output that is available at various price levels

2. Economic growth is most closely related to _____.
   A. business cycles
   B. long-term changes in the standard of living
   C. short-term changes in the standard of living
   D. day-to-day changes in business activity
   E. quarter-to-quarter changes in business activity

Economic Growth

Country	F	G	H	I	J
Population	100	10	40	50	60
Nominal GDP	$100,000	$15,000	$8,000	$80,000	$36,000
Price level	10	3	1	4	2

Use the table above to answer the following two questions.

3. Per capita real GDP in country I is _____.
   A. $100
   B. $200
   C. $300
   D. $400
   E. $500

4. The country with the highest level of per capita real GDP is country _____.
   A. F
   B. G
   C. H
   D. I
   E. J

5. A source of economic growth brought about by technological change is the _____.
   A. invention of the automobile
   B. discovery of petroleum reserves in Alaska
   C. increase in the population from 1900 to 1990
   D. increase in the number of women in the labor force
   E. increase in the number of teenagers in the labor force

6. In general, an economy that saves more today will _____.
   A. show an increase in consumption today
   B. show a decrease in consumption in the future
   C. be able to produce less real output in the future
   D. be able to produce more real output in the future
   E. cause the production possibilities curve to shift inward

7. Compared to more developed countries, less developed countries are often characterized by _____.
   A. political stability
   B. low levels of investment in research and development (R&D)
   C. high levels of educational attainment
   D. the production of many diversified products
   E. a stable financial and banking system

8. Compared to more developed countries, less developed countries are often characterized by _____.
   A. lower rates of population growth
   B. extensive transportation networks
   C. a system of unenforceable property rights
   D. wide public access to clean water and electricity
   E. low infant mortality rate

9. Compared to more developed countries, less developed countries are often characterized by _____.
   A. lower rates of population growth
   B. government corruption
   C. reliable information networks
   D. a smaller proportion of the labor force in agriculture
   E. high levels of foreign investment

10. To deal with the issues surrounding climate change, many economists advocate government implementation of _____.
    A. oil rationing
    B. laws making greenhouse gas emissions illegal
    C. market-based incentives to limit greenhouse emissions
    D. government regulation and ownership of coal power plants
    E. a price ceiling on oil to maintain low consumer prices

11. The problems encountered by transitional economies trying to become well-functioning market economies involve _____.
    A. eliminating bank checking accounts in favor of paper currency
    B. taking steps to raise the inflation rate
    C. expanding private property rights
    D. eliminating all welfare programs and social safety nets
    E. maintaining public perception that capitalism is evil

Short-answer essay questions.

12. Graphically illustrate how economic growth is portrayed in the AS/AD model.

13. List the pros and cons of international aid to developing countries.

14. Why is Russia encountering major obstacles to market reform?

15. Describe the relationship between long-run economic growth and the environment. How do a country's natural resources contribute to a nation's economy? Is the goal of long-run growth environmentally sustainable? Describe the policy options for dealing with environmental issues and the challenges in policy formation.

ANSWER KEY

1. C .... LO 1 .... Krugman/Wells, pp. 329–331; video segment 1
2. B .... LO 3 .... Krugman/Wells, pp. 226–227; video segment 1
3. D .... LO 3 .... Krugman/Wells, pp. 226–228
4. B .... LO 3 .... Krugman/Wells, pp. 226–228
5. A .... LO 2 .... Krugman/Wells, pp. 230–231; video segment 1
6. D .... LO 2 .... Krugman/Wells, p. 238; video segment 2
7. B .... LO 4 .... Krugman/Wells, pp. 238–241; video segment 4
8. C .... LO 4 .... Krugman/Wells, pp. 238–241; video segment 4
9. C .... LO 4 .... Krugman/Wells, pp. 238–241; video segment 4
10. C .... LO 7 .... Krugman/Wells, pp. 249–251; video segment 4
11. C .... LO 6 .... video segment 3

Short-answer essay questions.

12. LO 1 .... Krugman/Wells, pp. 329–331; video segment 1

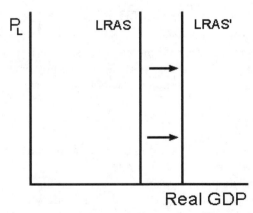

Economic growth is shown by a shift to the right of the long-run aggregate supply curve.

13. LO 5 .... video segment 4
The benefits of aid include reducing infant mortality rates; increasing access to potable water; and providing basic health services, sanitation improvements, and education.
The downside of aiding developing countries is inefficient distribution of aid and potential dependence on foreign aid.

14. LO 6.....................video segment 3

    Most of the Russian population had only experienced the Soviet system; therefore, capitalism was a new experience. Their culture, based on socialism and negative attitudes towards capitalism, has made the transition difficult. Declining infrastructure, political instability, currency fluctuations, and lack of laws protecting businesses are other factors that make the transition difficult.

15. LO 7.....................Krugman/Wells, pp. 235–236, 247–252

    Ceteris paribus, countries with greater natural resources have higher levels of per capita real GDP, but economic growth is also associated with increased degradation of the natural environment. The environmental issues facing today's international economy are global in scope and pose difficult challenges, especially with regards to energy generated from fossil fuels. Generally, economists believe that economic growth is sustainable even with the reality of limited and scarce natural resources because countries will innovate and find alternative ways of achieving growth and producing energy that minimize the impact of growth on the economy. Most economists agree that government intervention is required to deal with environmental issues as incentives are low for individuals to pay the cost today for solutions that are long-run environmentally sustainable. Government policy options include market-based incentives such as cap and trade pollution systems and carbon taxes. Challenges to policy formation include uncertainty about the size and scope of current environmental issues and the issue of international burden sharing.

LESSON INTERVIEWEES

Keishiro Ariizumi, Student, Dallas Japanese Society, Dallas, TX
J. Michael Finger, Lead Economist, The World Bank, Washington, DC
Jo Marie Greisgraber, Project Director, Rethinking Bretton Woods, Center of Concern, Washington, DC
Yuki Hou, Student, Dallas Japanese Society, Dallas, TX
Jeffrey Minsky, Chief Financial Officer, Protek Flagship Ltd., Pittsburgh, PA
David Ramsour, President, Texas Council of Economic Education, Houston, TX
Jorge A. Sanguinetty, Chairman, CEO, and President, DevTech Systems, Washington, DC
Philip Seib, Political Analyst, WFAA-TV, Dallas, TX
Shohei Takamatsu, Owner, Royal Tokyo Restaurant, Dallas, TX
Nobuo Tani, Assistant General Manager, NEC America, Inc., Dallas, TX
Wanda Tseng, Deputy Director, International Monetary Fund, Washington, DC

Lesson 8

The Nature of Money

OVERVIEW

This is a lesson that students usually enjoy, because it involves learning about "money." The lesson starts with a brief history of money, including a myriad of things that have been used as money over the centuries. Most of the examples chosen had problems associated with using the items as money. For instance, it was difficult to carry around bales of cotton or make change with diamonds. In our modern-day economy, there are still many different forms of money. The measurement of the different forms of money is highlighted in the video as M1, M2, and M3.

The third segment presents the creation of the Federal Reserve (commonly referred to as "the Fed") by Congress in 1913. The Federal Reserve has many responsibilities with the most important one being to maintain the stability of our money supply.

The next segment is the most challenging part of the lesson because of the complexity of the money creation process. Printing additional dollars is NOT the primary means of altering the money supply. The Treasury Department's Bureau of Engraving and Printing is responsible for the printing of our paper currency. The Federal Reserve puts these dollars into circulation to replace worn-out currency and to supply additional reserves when needed. Money is primarily created through loan-making activity, which creates more deposits and additional reserves, which leads to additional loan-making activity, additional deposits, additional reserves and so on. There is a limit to the loan-making ability and, therefore, money creation, from a change in reserves (R). This can be calculated with the deposit multiplier (m_d). Additional excess reserves (ER) multiplied by the reciprocal of the required reserve ratio (rr) is the maximum potential change in the money supply. Note: In the video, required reserve ratio is written as r.

The last segment focuses on the Federal Reserve's major responsibility of managing the money supply and the tools at its disposal to manipulate the money supply. The most frequently used tool of the Fed is open-market operations (OMO), the buying or selling of government securities. The Federal Open Market Committee (FOMC) determines the amount of securities that are bought or sold. It is important to note the Fed does not have complete control over the money supply. The behavior of banks and consumers can limit the Fed's ability to manipulate the economy through manipulation of the money supply. The Federal Reserve is a very powerful entity, and there is some disagreement about whether it should maintain its autonomy and power.

LESSON ASSIGNMENTS

Text: Krugman and Wells. *Macroeconomics*, Chapter 10, "Savings, Investment Spending, and the Financial System," pp. 271–276; Chapter 14, "Money, Banking, and the Federal Reserve System," pp. 381–413

Video: "The Nature of Money" from the series *Choices & Change: Macroeconomics*

LESSON OBJECTIVES

1. Define the following terms: *money, liquidity, financial intermediary, monetary base, central bank, leverage, balance sheet effect, subprime lending,* and *securitization*.

2. Explain the functions of money.

3. Distinguish between commodity money and fiat money.

4. Explain how each component of M1 and M2 meets the definition of money and performs the functions of money.

5. Distinguish the different characteristics of financial intermediaries.

6. Explain a fractional reserve banking system.

7. Interpret a T-account to identify assets and liabilities.

8. Use T-accounts to illustrate how banks can create or destroy money.

9. Calculate the deposit multiplier.

10. Describe the structure of the Fed.

11. Describe the functions of the Fed.

12. Describe the major tools of the Fed for altering the money supply.

13. Explain the advantages and disadvantages of having the Fed largely independent of the federal government.

14. Describe the different elements of the banking regulation system that have been designed to prevent bank runs.

15. Describe the causes of the 2008 financial crisis and the Fed's response to the crisis.

LESSON FOCUS POINTS

The following questions are designed to help you get the most benefit from the resources selected for this lesson. To maximize your learning experience:

    a. Scan the focus point questions.
    b. Read the assigned text pages.
    c. View the video.
    d. Write answers to the following questions. (References in parentheses can be used to locate information in the text and video that will help you answer the question.)

1. Choose three different items from the video "The Nature of Money" that have historically been used as a medium of exchange. Explain what makes each of these items less than desirable as a form of money. (video segment 2)

2. Briefly explain how currency performs the three functions of money. (textbook, p. 383; video segment 2)

3. How does commodity money differ from fiat money? Provide an example of commodity money and an example of fiat money. (textbook, pp. 384–385; video segment 2)

4. Explain what is meant by the term *liquidity*? Provide an example of an asset that is considered to be highly liquid and one that is not. What is the most liquid of all assets? (textbook, p. 273; video segment 2)

5. Definitions of money vary depending on their liquidity. List the components of the money supply from the most liquid to the least liquid. Explain the differences between M1 and M2. (textbook, pp. 385–386; video segment 2)

6. What are the functions of a financial intermediary? List four types of financial intermediaries. (textbook, pp. 275–276)

7. What are the major differences among the institutions you listed in the previous question? (textbook, pp. 275–276)

8. The United States operates with a fractional reserve banking system. Briefly explain how this system works and list the benefits of the system. (textbook, pp. 388–389; video segment 4)

9. Provide examples of assets and liabilities for a financial intermediary. Use a T-account to illustrate your examples. (textbook, pp. 388–389; video segment 4)

10. Assuming a required reserve ratio of 8 percent, use T-accounts to illustrate the money creation process initiated by an additional $10,000 of currency deposited into the banking system. Assume the following: (1) banks are currently fully loaned up, (2) banks choose to hold zero excess reserves (ER), and (3) there are no leakages into cash. Take the process through five loan creations. What would happen if the situation were reversed? (textbook, pp. 392–394; video segment 4)

11. Using the example in the previous question, what is the simple deposit multiplier? What is the maximum potential change in the money supply from the $10,000 deposit? (textbook, pp. 393–394; video segment 4)

12. Describe the structure of the Federal Reserve by addressing the following: (textbook, pp. 396–400; video segment 3)
    A. What is our nation's central bank?
    B. How many district banks does our central bank have?

Lesson 8—The Nature of Money

    C. How many members sit on the Board of Governors, how are they appointed, and how long do they serve?
    D. What is the purpose of the Federal Open Market Committee (FOMC) and who serves on this committee?
    E. Who owns the Federal Reserve District Banks?
    F. Are they in operation to make a profit?

13. The Federal Reserve's primary responsibility is to manage the nation's money supply. Briefly explain the other services the Fed provides to financial institutions. (textbook, pp. 396–397; video segment 3)

14. What are the three major tools of monetary policy? Briefly describe how each tool can change the money supply. (textbook, pp. 397–399; video segment 5)

15. In the video "The Nature of Money," what are the arguments for and against having an independent Federal Reserve System? (video segments 3 and 5)

16. What are the elements of the banking regulation system that help to prevent bank runs? What role does the discount window play in preventing bank runs? Who provides deposit insurance? (textbook, pp. 390–391)

17. What events led to the 2008 financial crisis? What was the role of subprime mortgage lending and securitization? What was the Fed's response to the crisis? What are the potential future repercussions? (textbook, pp. 406–409)

REVIEW

The following process is intended to help you retain the knowledge you have acquired in this lesson.

- Review key points in the "Quick Reviews" at the end of each section in the textbook.
- Complete the "Check Your Understanding" questions at the end of each section and check your answers using the answer key at the end of the textbook.
- Review the case studies in "Economics in Action" in the textbook.
- Review the critical concepts noted in the page margins of the textbook.
- Complete the following Practice Test and check your responses.
- Revisit the text and/or video for any questions you answer incorrectly on the Practice Test.

PRACTICE TEST

Multiple Choice: Circle the letter that corresponds to the BEST answer for each question.

1. Money is anything that _____.
   A. can be converted into gold with relatively little loss in value
   B. can be converted into silver with relatively little loss in value
   C. serves as a medium of exchange for goods and services
   D. facilitates a connecting link between credit instruments and debt instruments
   E. facilitates the wholesaling or retailing of funds

2. Inflation of the general price level reduces the ability of money to function as a _____.
   A. medium of exchange
   B. medium of value
   C. unit of account
   D. standard of deferred payment
   E. store of value

3. The unit-of-account function means money is used _____.
   A. as a consistent means of measuring the value of things
   B. as the common denominator of future payments
   C. to pay for goods and services
   D. to accumulate purchasing power
   E. to facilitate a double coincidence of wants

4. Money that has value apart from its use as money is _____.
   A. fiat money
   B. currency
   C. convertible paper money
   D. private debt money
   E. commodity money

5. The ease in which an asset can be exchanged for currency represents _____.
   A. M1
   B. reserves
   C. liabilities
   D. liquidity
   E. M2

6. The largest component of M1 is _____.
   A. currency
   B. treasury bonds
   C. checkable deposits
   D. savings deposits
   E. time deposits

Lesson 8—The Nature of Money

7. A classification of money that is included in M2 but not in M1 is _____.
   A. currency
   B. demand deposits
   C. banker's acceptances
   D. traveler's checks
   E. time deposits

8. An institution that collects funds from lenders and distributes these funds to borrowers is _____.
   A. a financial intermediary
   B. the Federal Reserve System
   C. a wholesale store
   D. a retail store
   E. the Federal Deposit Insurance Corporation

9. The principle of fractional reserve banking makes it possible for a _____.
   A. bank to make loans
   B. bank to print currency
   C. bank to avoid reserve requirements
   D. goldsmith to print currency
   E. goldsmith to establish the gold standard

Components of the Money System
(in billions of dollars)

Currency	$100
Checkable deposits	300
Traveler's checks	50
Savings deposits	75
Money market funds	500
Time deposits	800
Other less liquid assets	125

Use the table above to answer the following two questions.

10. The money supply measured by M2 is _____.
    A. $450 billion
    B. $1,025 billion
    C. $1,825 billion
    D. $1,950 billion
    E. $2,200 billion

11. The difference between M1 and M2 is _____.
    A. $325 billion
    B. $450 billion
    C. $575 billion
    D. $1,375 billion
    E. $1,500 billion

12. The law requires banks to maintain _____.
    A. fractional reserves in the form of deposit liabilities against their liquid assets
    B. fractional reserves in the form of federal securities against their outstanding loans
    C. fractional reserves in the form of liquid assets against their deposit liabilities
    D. legal reserves in the form of gold against their outstanding loans
    E. legal reserves equal to their net worth

13. Which of the following are bank reserves?
    A. Demand deposits with other banks
    B. Deposits with the Federal Reserve
    C. Treasury bonds and bills
    D. State bonds of the state in which the bank is located but not state bonds of other states
    E. State bonds of any and all states in the United States

14. A bank is fully loaned up when _____.
    A. legal reserves are zero
    B. excess reserves are zero
    C. primary reserves are zero
    D. required reserves are zero
    E. nonlegal reserves are zero

15. Assume that all banks in the banking system are fully loaned up and that the required reserve ratio is 20 percent. If one bank obtains excess reserves of $10,000, then checkable deposits could ultimately increase by _____.
    A. $10,000
    B. $20,000
    C. $30,000
    D. $40,000
    E. $50,000

16. To reduce the political influence of the Board of Governors, _____.
    A. the president appoints a new board every 4 years
    B. the president appoints a new board every 8 years
    C. the reelection campaign for each member is less than 1 year
    D. each member is appointed for 7 years, with one term expiring every year
    E. each member is appointed for 14 years

17. A primary function of a central bank is to _____.
    A. regulate dividend payments by corporations
    B. control the bond market
    C. set monetary policy
    D. publish statistics on banking and related financial matters
    E. determine the international balance of payments

18. Federal Reserve Banks are owned by _____.
    A. their member banks
    B. Wall Street investors
    C. the Board of Governors
    D. the U.S. Treasury
    E. the Bank of the United States

19. Assume that the banking system has $10,000 in deposits and $1,000 in reserves. If the required reserve ratio changes from 10 percent to 5 percent _____.
    A. reserves will decrease to $500
    B. excess reserves will increase to $500
    C. required reserves will increase to $1,000
    D. total deposits in the banking system will ultimately decline
    E. banks must transfer $500 of nonlegal reserves into legal reserves

20. The most important tool of monetary policy for achieving economic stabilization is _____.
    A. moral suasion
    B. reserve ratios
    C. the discount rate
    D. margin requirements
    E. open-market operations

21. Which of the following is NOT used to help prevent bank runs?
    A. Deposit insurance
    B. Capital requirements
    C. Leverage requirements
    D. Reserve requirements
    E. Discount window

22. The rate of interest that banks charge to loan their excess reserves to other banks is the _____.
    A. federal funds rate
    B. required reserve rate
    C. discount rate
    D. capital rate
    E. deposit rate

23. A bank that borrows money to finance investments is participating in _____.
    A. leverage
    B. securitization
    C. the balance sheet effect
    D. subprime lending
    E. open-market operations

24. _____ occurs when loans are grouped together in a pool and then sold in shares to investors.
    A. Leverage
    B. Securitization
    C. The balance sheet effect
    D. Subprime lending
    E. The cycle of deleveraging

Short-answer essay questions.

25. List three different types of financial intermediaries and their characteristics.

26. Use T-accounts to illustrate money creation from an increase in excess reserves of $20,000 with a required reserve ratio of 10 percent.

27. What is the potential maximum increase in the money supply from the previous question?

28. List the major functions of the Federal Reserve Banks.

29. Do you think the Federal Reserve Banks should retain their autonomous standing? Why?

30. What were the primary causes of the 2008 financial crisis? What action did the Fed take in response to the crisis and how has this affected its balance sheet?

ANSWER KEY

1. C .... LO 1 .... Krugman/Wells, p. 382; video segment 2
2. E .... LO 2 .... Krugman/Wells, p. 383; video segment 2
3. A .... LO 2 .... Krugman/Wells, p. 383; video segment 2
4. E .... LO 3 .... Krugman/Wells, pp. 384–385; video segment 2
5. D .... LO 1 .... Krugman/Wells, p. 273; video segment 2
6. A .... LO 4 .... Krugman/Wells, p. 386; video segment 2
7. E .... LO 4 .... Krugman/Wells, pp. 385–386
8. A .... LO 1 .... Krugman/Wells, pp. 275, 388; video segment 4
9. A .... LO 6 .... Krugman/Wells, pp. 388–389; video segment 4
10. C .... LO 4 .... Krugman/Wells, p. 386
11. D .... LO 4 .... Krugman/Wells, p. 386
12. C .... LO 6 .... Krugman/Wells, pp. 388–389; video segment 4
13. B .... LO 6 .... Krugman/Wells, p. 388; video segment 4
14. B .... LO 6 .... Krugman/Wells, pp. 393–394; video segment 4
15. E .... LO 9 .... Krugman/Wells, pp. 392–394; video segment 4
16. E .... LO 10 .... Krugman/Wells, p. 396; video segment 4
17. C .... LO 11 .... Krugman/Wells, p. 396; video segment 3
18. A .... LO 10 .... video segment 3
19. B .... LO 12 .... Krugman/Wells, pp. 393–394, 397–398; video segment 4
20. E .... LO 12 .... Krugman/Wells, p. 398; video segment 5

21. C .... LO 14 .... Krugman/Wells, pp. 397–398
22. A .... LO 12 .... Krugman/Wells, pp. 397–398
23. A .... LO 1 .... Krugman/Wells, pp. 406–408
24. B .... LO 1 .... Krugman/Wells, pp. 406–407

Short-answer essay questions.

25. LO 5 .... Krugman/Wells, pp. 275–276
    Financial intermediaries accept deposits from certain groups and offer loans to others. The most important intermediaries are commercial banks. The main characteristic that sets banks apart from other intermediaries is that they are allowed to offer checkable deposits. Insurance companies and pension funds are also financial intermediaries; however, they do not offer checking accounts.

26. LO 7, 8 .... Krugman/Wells, pp. 392–394; video segment 4

Bank A

Assets		Liabilities
Reserves +20,000 (ER 18,000)		+20,000 deposit
Reserves 2,000 Loans 18,000		

Bank B

Assets		Liabilities
Reserves +18,000 (ER 16,200)		+18,000 deposit
Reserves 1,800 Loans 16,200		

Bank C

Assets		Liabilities
Reserves +16,200 (ER 14,580)		+16,200 deposit
Reserves 1,620 Loans 14,580		

Bank D

Assets		Liabilities
Reserves +14,580 (ER 13,122)		+14,580 deposit
Reserves 1,458 Loans 13,122		

If we assume that banks wish to hold no excess reserves, then the loan-making activity will continue as long as there are excess reserves (ER).

27. LO 8, 9.................Krugman/Wells, pp. 393–394; video segment 4
    The maximum potential change in the money supply is found by multiplying (ER) times the simple deposit multiplier (1/rr).

    ER(1/rr) =

    18,000 (1/.10) = $180,000

28. LO 11.................Krugman/Wells, pp. 396–399; video segment 3
    In addition to their main function of maintaining the stability of the money supply, the Federal Reserve Banks also:
    A. provide check clearing services.
    B. act as fiscal agents for the U.S. Treasury.
    C. are lenders of last resort.
    D. are bank regulators.

29. LO 13.................video segments 3 and 5
    The answer to this question is based on your opinions. Make sure you have included the basis for your opinion.

30. LO 15.................Kurgman/Wells, pp. 406–409
    Low interest rates in the early 2000s led to a housing boom and a large increase in risky subprime mortgage lending. The risks of these loans were then spread throughout the international financial system through the process of securitization. When housing prices fell and borrowers were unable to pay their loans, financial institutions were unable to recoup their losses and investors began to lose confidence in the financial system. This led to a cycle of deleveraging and a frozen credit market as limited credit availability led many financial institutions into crisis and put them on the verge of failing. The Fed responded to the crisis in several ways, helping to rescue financial institutions considered too large to fail and purchasing private debt from troubled institutions. The Fed has also made additional funds available for troubled financial institutions. As a result of these measures, the Fed now holds a wide variety of risky assets usually not found on its balance sheet and is exposed to a higher level of risk than at other times in its history.

LESSON INTERVIEWEES

Jeff Carbiener, Adjunct Professor of Economics, Southern Methodist University, Dallas, TX
Stan Carnes, Managing Director, Salomon Smith Barney, New York City, NY
Howard Hamilton, Executive Vice-President, McIlroy Bank and Trust Company, Fayetteville, AR
Steve Malin, Assistant Vice-President, Media Relations Officer and Senior Economist, Federal Reserve Bank of New York, New York, NY
Duane Rosa, Professor of Economics, West Texas A&M University, Canyon, TX
Philip Seib, Political Analyst, WFAA-TV, Dallas, TX
Ed Stevens, Senior Consultant and Economist, Federal Reserve Bank of Cleveland, Cleveland, OH

Lesson 9

Financial Markets

OVERVIEW

This lesson brings financial markets into the picture. Interest rates, bond prices, currency exchange rates, and other financial aspects directly and indirectly affect the macroeconomy. U.S. government bonds and the inverse relationship that exists between bond prices and interest rates are presented. U.S. bonds are generally considered to be "risk free," which explains the lower yields on these instruments. Just how risk free these securities are was questioned in 1995 when the government ran out of funds and had an interest payment due. This created the possibility of default; however, the markets did not show much reaction. The government shut down nonessential activities for approximately three weeks, the interest payment was made, and life went back to normal. When the market for bonds is in motion, supply and demand analysis is useful in analyzing the price changes. Price changes in turn change the yields or interest on these bonds. This segment also addresses the international effects of changes in the bond markets.

The third segment focuses on currency markets. The demand for U.S. government bonds by foreigners is related to the demand for U.S. dollars. Again supply and demand analysis is used to examine how changes in the market cause changes in currency prices. Governments sometimes take actions that directly affect currency markets and prices. This segment also illustrates why there is a demand for foreign currencies. For example, importing and exporting usually require currency exchange; tourism and investors seeking out the best return versus risk may need foreign currency to buy foreign bonds. The introduction of the Euro is also explored in this segment.

The demand for money can be separated into 3 different categories. First and foremost is the demand for liquid assets in order to buy goods and services. This is often called transactions demand for money. Precautionary demand is keeping liquid assets in case of unexpected expenses, such as car repairs or medical costs. The need for liquid assets, in case an "opportunity" comes along, is the speculative demand for money.

The next segment illustrates how financial markets cause changes in interest rates, which cause changes in spending, which then cause changes in aggregate demand. Changes in interest rates have a double effect on aggregate demand. Not only does business investment change due to interest rate changes, but consumer spending that depends on interest rates also changes.

How bond markets, currency markets, and money markets are interrelated and how they affect the macroeconomy are the focuses of the last part of this video.

LESSON ASSIGNMENTS

Text: Krugman and Wells. *Macroeconomics*, Chapter 15, "Monetary Policy," pp. 415–442; Chapter 18, "Open-Economy Macroeconomics," pp. 493–524

Video: "Financial Markets" from the series *Choices & Change: Macroeconomics*

LESSON OBJECTIVES

1. Recognize the inverse relationship between interest rates and bond prices.

2. Explain why an increase in bond prices might result in an increase in aggregate demand and vice versa.

3. Explain why foreigners might want domestic currency and why locals might want foreign currency.

4. Explain how a change in the interest rate of a country might affect the demand for its currency.

5. Explain how a change in the exchange rate or in interest rates might affect aggregate demand.

6. Describe the factors that affect how much money people wish to hold.

7. Explain the graph of money supply.

8. Define money market equilibrium.

9. Explain what causes movement toward equilibrium in the money market when the actual interest rate is above or below its equilibrium level.

10. Interpret graphs of aggregate supply and demand that display the effects of changes in the money supply.

LESSON FOCUS POINTS

The following questions are designed to help you get the most benefit from the resources selected for this lesson. To maximize your learning experience:

    a. Scan the focus point questions.
    b. Read the assigned text pages.
    c. View the video.
    d. Write answers to the following questions. (References in parentheses can be used to locate information in the text and video that will help you answer the question.)

1. What causes bond prices to change? Explain why interest rates go down when bond prices rise and why bond prices fall when interest rates go up. (video segment 2)

2. Briefly explain how a change in bond prices affects investment and aggregate demand. Explain the process for both an increase and a decrease in bond prices. (video segment 2)

3. Why are there currency markets? Who are the suppliers and who are the demanders of currencies? (textbook, pp. 504–505; video segment 3)

4. Financial capital will flow to where it can get the highest return for a given level of risk. If interest rates are higher in the United States than in Japan, what will holders of financial capital in Japan do? Will this situation increase or decrease the demand for U.S. dollars? How will this example affect currency markets? (textbook, pp. 498–501; video segment 3)

5. Using supply and demand analysis, what are two ways the dollar can appreciate (increase in value)? What effect will an appreciating dollar have on the volume of imports and exports and therefore aggregate demand? Using supply and demand analysis, what are two ways the dollar can depreciate (decrease in value)? What effect will a depreciating dollar have on the volume of imports and exports and therefore aggregate demand? (textbook, pp. 504–510; video segment 3)

6. Define the demand for money. What factors affect the quantities of money people choose to hold? (textbook, pp. 416–421; video segment 4)

7. Construct a graph of the money supply. Briefly explain the shape of the money supply curve. What factors cause this curve to shift? (textbook, pp. 421–422; video segment 4)

8. Graphically illustrate and explain money market equilibrium. (textbook, pp. 421–422; video segment 4)

9. When interest rates are above the money market equilibrium interest rate, what will happen to move interest rates toward equilibrium? When interest rates are below the money market equilibrium interest rate, what will happen to move interest rates toward equilibrium? (textbook, pp. 421–422; video segments 4 and 5)

10. Using the AS/AD model, graphically illustrate and then explain how changes in the money supply affect interest rates and, subsequently, aggregate demand. (textbook, pp. 421–428; video segment 4)

REVIEW

The following process is intended to help you retain the knowledge you have acquired in this lesson.

- Review key points in the "Quick Reviews" at the end of each section in the textbook.
- Complete the "Check Your Understanding" questions at the end of each section and check your answers using the answer key at the end of the textbook.
- Review the case studies in "Economics in Action" in the textbook.
- Review the critical concepts noted in the page margins of the textbook.
- Complete the following Practice Test and check your responses.
- Revisit the text and/or video for any questions you answer incorrectly on the Practice Test.

PRACTICE TEST

Multiple Choice: Circle the letter that corresponds to the BEST answer for each question.

The Bond Market

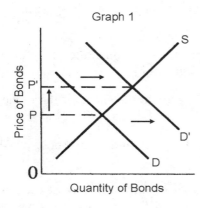
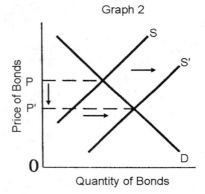

Use the graphs above to answer the following two questions.

1. Given the bond market illustrated in Graph 1, the interest rate will _____.
   A. increase
   B. decrease
   C. remain unchanged
   D. increase then return to the original level
   E. decrease then return to the original level

2. Given the bond market illustrated in Graph 2, the interest rate will _____ and business investment will _____.
   A. increase; increase
   B. increase; decrease
   C. decrease; increase
   D. decrease; decrease
   E. increase; remain unchanged

3. An increase in the demand for bonds generates _____ in the interest rate and _____ in aggregate demand.
   A. an increase; an increase
   B. an increase; a decrease
   C. a decrease; an increase
   D. a decrease; a decrease
   E. no change; no change

4. A decrease in the demand for domestic bonds generates _____ in the domestic interest rate and _____ in the exchange rate. (The exchange rate is calculated as the foreign currency/domestic currency.)
   A. an increase; an increase
   B. an increase; a decrease
   C. a decrease; an increase
   D. a decrease; a decrease
   E. no change; no change

5. If the U.S. exchange rate increases relative to currencies in other countries, then the United States _____. (The exchange rate is calculated as the foreign currency/domestic currency.)
   A. imports and exports will both increase
   B. imports and exports will both decrease
   C. imports will decrease and exports will increase
   D. imports will increase and exports will decrease
   E. imports and exports will not change

6. If the exchange rate moves from €1.50 per US$1 to €1.35 per US$1, the euro has _____ and European exports to the United States will _____.
   A. depreciated; increase
   B. depreciated; decrease
   C. appreciated; increase
   D. appreciated; decrease
   E. not changed in value; decrease

7. The money households and firms hold in order to pay for the goods and services they buy is the _____.
   A. velocity demand
   B. precautionary demand
   C. transactions demand
   D. transfer demand
   E. speculative demand

8. The money households and firms hold because of a concern that bond prices and the prices of other financial assets might fall is the _____.
   A. velocity demand
   B. precautionary demand
   C. transactions demand
   D. transfer demand
   E. speculative demand

9. The slope of the supply curve of money is _____.
   A. vertical
   B. horizontal
   C. zero
   D. negative
   E. U-shaped

Monetary Policy and the AD-SRAS Model

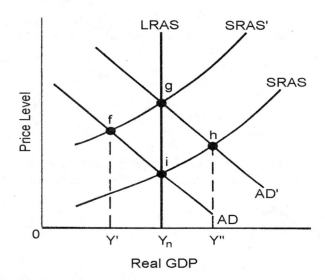

Use the graph above to answer the following question.

10. An increase in the money supply is most likely to cause a shift _____.
    A. from SRAS to SRAS'
    B. from AD to AD'
    C. from SRAS' to SRAS
    D. from AD' to AD
    E. of the LRAS curve

11. The interaction among institutions through which money is supplied to individuals, firms, and other institutions that demand money is the _____.
    A. transfer market
    B. velocity of money market
    C. exchange market
    D. currency market
    E. money market

12. Money market equilibrium occurs at the interest rate at which the _____.
    A. quantity of money demanded is equal to the quantity of money supplied
    B. quantity of money demanded is less than the quantity of money supplied
    C. quantity of money demanded is greater than the quantity of money supplied
    D. slopes of the demand curve for money and the supply curve for money are equal
    E. demand curve for money and the supply curve for money are tangent

13. An increase in the supply of money, with no change in the demand for money, will lead to _____ in equilibrium quantity of money and _____ in equilibrium interest rate.
    A. an increase; an increase
    B. an increase; a decrease
    C. a decrease; an increase
    D. a decrease; a decrease
    E. no change; no change

14. In the short-run, an increase in the supply of money will lead to _____ in equilibrium real GDP and _____ in equilibrium interest rate.
    A. an increase; an increase
    B. an increase; a decrease
    C. a decrease; an increase
    D. a decrease; a decrease
    E. no change; no change

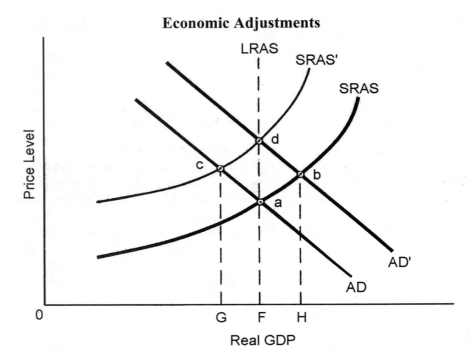

Use the graph above to answer the following question.

15. Assume that the economy is at point b. A decrease in the money supply would cause _____.

    A. a shift of the SRAS curve to SRAS'
    B. a shift of the SRAS' curve to SRAS
    C. a shift of the AD curve to AD'
    D. a shift of the AD' curve to AD
    E. no change in the AD or SRAS curves

Short-answer essay questions.

16. Based on the video "Financial Markets," what stimulates the demand for foreign currency?

17. Graphically illustrate and explain how the money market seeks equilibrium.

ANSWER KEY

1. B .... LO 1 .... video segment 2
2. B .... LO 1, 2 .... video segment 2
3. C .... LO 1, 2 .... video segment 2
4. A .... LO 1, 3, 4 ... video segment 3
5. D .... LO 5 .... Krugman/Wells, pp. 505–508; video segments 3 and 4
6. D .... LO 5 .... Krugman/Wells, pp. 504–507
7. C .... LO 6 .... Wyatt, student course guide Lesson 9 Overview
8. E .... LO 6 .... Wyatt, student course guide Lesson 9 Overview
9. A .... LO 7 .... Krugman/Wells, pp. 421–422; video segments 3 and 4
10. B .... LO 10 .... Krugman/Wells, pp. 426–427; video segment 4
11. E .... LO 8 .... Krugman/Wells, pp. 421–422
12. A .... LO 8 .... Krugman/Wells, pp. 421–422; video segment 4
13. B .... LO 8, 9 .... Krugman/Wells, p. 423; video segment 4
14. B .... LO 10 .... Krugman/Wells, pp. 423, 432; video segment 4
15. D .... LO 10 .... Krugman/Wells, pp. 423–424, 426, 432; video segment 4

Short-answer essay questions.

16. LO 3, 4 .... Krugman/Wells, pp. 504–505; video segment 3
    In the video "Financial Markets," there are several reasons for demanding foreign currency.
    A. Financial investment flows to the highest interest rates per a given level of risk. If that is in a foreign country, that currency is needed to buy those bonds.
    B. Tourists require foreign currencies.
    C. Importers and exporters have a need for currency markets.

17. LO 9 .... Krugman/Wells, pp. 421–422; video segment 3

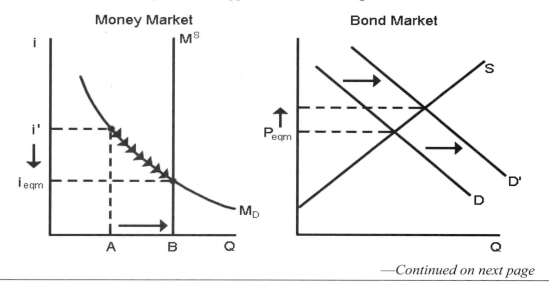

—Continued on next page

Lesson 9—Financial Markets

If interest rates are i', then the quantity demanded of money (A) is less than the quantity supplied (B), resulting in a surplus of money. Because of higher interest rates, money flows into bonds, increasing the demand for bonds. This demand increase drives up the price of bonds and decreases market interest rates. This activity will continue, *ceteris paribus*, as long as market interest rates exceed equilibrium interest rates.

LESSON INTERVIEWEES

Kari Battaglia, Lecturer, Department of Economics, University of North Texas, Denton, TX
Sam F. Ciccarello, General Manager, Vigo Importing Company, Tampa, FL
George Friedlander, Managing Director—Fixed Income Strategist, Salomon Smith Barney, New York City, NY
William C. Gruben, Chief International Economist, Federal Reserve Bank of Dallas, Dallas, TX
David Johnson, Stockbroker, Dallas, TX
James A. Kornegay Jr., Tourist, Allen, TX
Dr. Magnus L. Kpakol, Business Economist and Adjunct Professor of Economics, University of North Texas, Denton, TX and University of Dallas, Irving, TX
Steve Malin, Assistant Vice-President, Media Relations Officer and Senior Economist, Federal Reserve Bank of New York, New York, NY
Robert D. McTeer Jr., President and CEO, Federal Reserve Bank of Dallas, Dallas, TX
Louis Richard, Sector Manager, Cargill, Inc., Tampa, FL
Philip Seib, Political Analyst, WFAA-TV, Dallas, TX

Lesson 10

Monetary Policy

OVERVIEW

Now that you have learned about money creation and the structure of the Federal Reserve System, it is time to look at the Fed's use of discretionary monetary policy to influence the macroeconomy. Recall the tools available for the Fed's use in stabilizing the economy: open-market operations, the discount rate, and the reserve ratio. This lesson focuses on how these tools can alter the macroeconomy and on the problems associated with using these tools to contract or expand the economy.

When the economy is in a recession, the Fed may engage in discretionary expansionary monetary policy. Usually the goal is to increase aggregate demand by increasing consumer or business spending (investment), which should move the economy toward full employment equilibrium. Historically, the Federal Reserve's actions to reduce or control inflation have often been more effective than its actions to stimulate the economy. Reducing the money supply and the subsequent increase in interest rates is usually very effective at reducing economic activity. Segment 3 also illustrates the effect of monetary policy on business decisions. You should be able to utilize the information in the video to draw an AS/AD graph explaining how monetary policy could affect the economy. This segment also presents some of the problems associated with discretionary monetary policy. What measures should the Fed target: Federal funds rate, M1, or M2? Time lags associated with monetary policy, as well as not having control over consumer or business behavior, are additional problems that limit the ability of the Fed to keep the economy at full employment.

Both fiscal and monetary policies are subject to time lags that may affect their efficacy. First there is the recognition lag (data lag) where it may be three to six months before the statistics show a problem. Next is the legislative (political) lag where fiscal policy in particular must go through the legislative process. Then there are implementation and impact lags because it takes time for the multiplied process of either fiscal or monetary policy to work its way through the economy. The major problem with these lags is that the economic situation the policy was designed to fix may have already corrected itself and the policies could create the opposite problem.

As seen in the video, an especially difficult time for many people was the *stagflation* period in the 1970s and early 1980s. Stagflation represents an economy that is in a recession and therefore experiencing high rates of unemployment; however, the economy was also experiencing high rates of inflation. This time period was an exception to the fixed Phillips curve's inverse relationship between inflation and unemployment. Monetary policy that changed aggregate demand would have been inappropriate in this instance. Typically, if AD increases, then unemployment decreases, but price levels rise. If monetary policy decreases AD, then price levels fall, but unemployment rises. Therefore, any monetary policy that affects AD improves one problem (inflation or unemployment) while making the other one worse.

Segment 4 illustrates the equation of exchange MV = PY (M = money supply, V = velocity, P = price level, Y = real GDP) and explains the concept of velocity and how velocity is determined. Some economists use Q to represent real GDP; therefore, the equation of exchange is sometimes represented as MV = PQ. There is disagreement over whether velocity is stable or variable. This question is important because the answer affects the ability of monetary policy to influence the macroeconomy.

LESSON ASSIGNMENTS

Text: Krugman and Wells, *Macroeconomics*, Chapter 6, "Macroeconomics: The Big Picture," p. 156; Chapter 11, "Income and Expenditure," pp. 298–299; Chapter 12, "Aggregate Demand and Aggregate Supply," pp. 320–323, 338–341; Chapter 13, "Fiscal Policy," pp.358–359; Chapter 14, "Money, Banking, and the Federal Reserve System," pp. 397–399; Chapter 15, "Monetary Policy," pp.415–442; Chapter 17, "Macroeconomics: Events and Ideas," pp.481–482

Video: "Monetary Policy" from the series *Choices & Change: Macroeconomics*

LESSON OBJECTIVES

1. Define monetary policy.

2. Describe the goals of monetary policy.

3. List and define the policy tools of the Fed.

4. Describe the different policy implementation rules that a central bank can use.

5. Explain and illustrate how the policy tools of the Fed are supposed to affect economic activity.

6. Explain monetary policy lags.

7. Explain the rational expectations model.

8. Explain the potential effect of the rational expectations model on the effectiveness of monetary policy.

9. Draw a graph to illustrate how monetary policy can be offset by changes in investment.

10. Explain factors that determine velocity of money.

LESSON FOCUS POINTS

The following questions are designed to help you get the most benefit from the resources selected for this lesson. To maximize your learning experience:

   a. Scan the focus point questions.
   b. Read the assigned text pages.
   c. View the video.
   d. Write answers to the following questions. (References in parentheses can be used to locate information in the text and video that will help you answer the question.)

1. What is monetary policy and who is responsible for conducting it? (textbook, pp. 156, 426–427; video segment 1)

2. What are the primary goals of monetary policy? Why are they important? (textbook, pp. 426–429; video segment 2)

3. Explain what tools of monetary policy the Fed can use to increase the money supply. Why would the Fed take these actions? (textbook, pp. 323, 338–341, 397–399, 426–429; video segment 2)

4. If the Fed chose to decrease the money supply, explain what actions the Fed would take. What are the advantages and disadvantages of each tool of monetary policy? (textbook, pp. 397–399, 421–425; video segment 2)

5. Draw an aggregate supply and an aggregate demand curve. Also draw a graph of the money market. Show graphically what will happen if the Fed pursues expansionary monetary policies. Draw another set of curves and show graphically what will happen if the Fed pursues contractionary policies. (textbook, pp. 423–427; video segment 2)

6. What factors can stall or delay the expected actions from monetary policies? (textbook, pp. 481–482; student course guide Lesson 10 Overview; video segment 3)

7. Timing may be a problem in using monetary policy as a stabilization tool. The lags that may hinder the effectiveness of monetary policy as a stabilization tool are recognition, implementation, and impact lag. Explain the causes of these lags and briefly state how they could impair the effectiveness of monetary policy. (student course guide Lesson 10 Overview; video segment 3)

8. What is the basic premise of the rational expectations hypothesis? (textbook, pp. 481–482 ; video segment 3)

9. Provide an example of how rational expectations may render monetary policies useless or ineffective in achieving their purpose. (textbook, pp. 481–482; video segment 3)

10. Construct a graph of investment demand and an AS/AD graph. Show graphically and briefly explain how changes in investment can offset the effects of expansionary monetary policy. (video segment 3)

11. The following equation is referred to as the equation of exchange MV=PY. Define each of the variables in this equation and identify the factors that affect velocity and how they affect velocity. (student course guide Lesson 10 Overview; video segment 4)

REVIEW

The following process is intended to help you retain the knowledge you have acquired in this lesson.

- Review key points in the "Quick Reviews" at the end of each section in the textbook.
- Complete the "Check Your Understanding" questions at the end of each section and check your answers using the answer key at the end of the textbook.
- Review the case studies in "Economics in Action" in the textbook.
- Review the critical concepts noted in the page margins of the textbook.
- Complete the following Practice Test and check your responses.
- Revisit the text and/or video for any questions you answer incorrectly on the Practice Test.

PRACTICE TEST

Multiple Choice: Circle the letter that corresponds to the BEST answer for each question.

1. A primary goal of monetary policy is to _____.
    A. maintain high interest rates
    B. eliminate trade barriers from other nations
    C. prevent high rates of inflation
    D. reduce the size of the banking sector
    E. limit the availability of consumer credit

2. _____ is NOT one of the Fed's primary goals in conducting monetary policy.
    A. Zero inflation
    B. Price stability
    C. Low unemployment
    D. Smoothing the business cycle
    E. Economic growth

3. The tool of monetary policy that involves the Fed's buying and selling of government securities is _____.
    A. moral suasion
    B. reserve requirements
    C. the discount rate
    D. margin requirements
    E. open-market operations

4. In principle, if the Fed wants to reduce the money supply by discouraging depository institutions from borrowing reserves from Federal Reserve Banks, it could use _____.
   A. moral suasion
   B. reserve requirements
   C. the discount rate
   D. margin requirements
   E. open-market operations

5. If the Fed pursues policy that leads to a decrease in interest rates, investment spending will _____, shifting the aggregate demand curve to the _____.
   A. not change; right
   B. increase; left
   C. decrease; left
   D. increase; right
   E. decrease; right

6. If the economy is in a recessionary gap, the Fed should pursue _____ monetary policy, which would shift the aggregate demand curve to the _____.
   A. expansionary; left
   B. contractionary; left
   C. expansionary; right
   D. contractionary; right
   E. inflationary; right

7. When actual real GDP is greater than potential real GDP and the central bank is concerned about rising inflation, it could _____ government securities to pursue the appropriate _____ monetary policy.
   A. create; contractionary
   B. buy; expansionary
   C. sell; contractionary
   D. buy; inflationary
   E. sell; expansionary

8. The delay between the time at which an event occurs and the time at which policymakers become aware of it is the _____.
   A. impact lag
   B. political lag
   C. implementation lag
   D. government lag
   E. recognition lag

9. The use of all available information to forecast future levels of economic activity and adjust behavior accordingly is _____.
   A. monetary policy
   B. fiscal policy
   C. recognition policy
   D. rational expectations
   E. liquidity

10. According to the principle of monetary neutrality, a change in the money supply results in a long-run change in _____.
    A. interest rates
    B. real GDP
    C. the federal funds rate
    D. the price level
    E. all of the above

11. If the central bank sets monetary policy to attain a specified inflation rate, it is utilizing _____.
    A. expansionary monetary policy
    B. inflation targeting
    C. monetary neutrality
    D. contractionary monetary policy
    E. the Taylor rule

12. When the Fed sets a target federal funds rate based on the inflation rate and the gap between potential and actual real GDP, it is employing _____.
    A. expansionary monetary policy
    B. inflation targeting
    C. monetary neutrality
    D. contractionary monetary policy
    E. the Taylor rule

13. When consumers and businesses utilize all available information and adjust their behavior accordingly, the result affects the ability of monetary policy to stabilize the economy. This refers to _____.
    A. monetarism
    B. the rational expectations theory
    C. classical theory
    D. all of the above
    E. none of the above

14. If V = 5, M = $200, and P = $2, then Y is _____.
    A. 10
    B. 40
    C. 400
    D. 500
    E. 1,000

Short-answer essay questions.

15. What is monetary policy, and who is responsible for implementing monetary policy?

16. Graphically illustrate and explain how expansionary monetary policy should affect the macroeconomy.

17. Continue with the example in question 16. Illustrate the effect of pessimistic business expectations on the effects of the expansionary monetary policy.

ANSWER KEY

1. C .... LO 2 .... Krugman/Wells, pp. 428–429; video segment 2
2. A .... LO 2 .... Krugman/Wells, pp. 426–429
3. E .... LO 3 .... Krugman/Wells, pp. 398–399; video segment 2
4. C .... LO 3 .... Krugman/Wells, pp. 397–398
5. D .... LO 2, 5 .... Krugman/Wells, pp. 298–299, 322
6. C .... LO 2, 5 .... Krugman/Wells, pp. 426–427
7. C .... LO 2, 5 .... Krugman/Wells, pp. 426–429
8. E .... LO 6 .... Wyatt student course guide Lesson 10 Overview
9. D .... LO 7 .... Krugman/Wells, pp. 481–482; video segment 3
10. D .... LO 5 .... Krugman/Wells, p. 433
11. B .... LO 4 .... Krugman/Wells, pp. 428–429
12. E .... LO 4 .... Krugman/Wells, pp. 428–429
13. B .... LO 8 .... Krugman/Wells, pp. 481–482; video segment 3
14. D .... LO 10 .... Wyatt student course guide Lesson 10 Overview; video segment 4

Short-answer essay questions.

15. LO 1 .... Krugman/Wells, pp. 156, 396–397; video segment 1
    Monetary policy is money and credit controls carried out by the Federal Reserve in order to encourage economic growth while maintaining price stability and low levels of unemployment.

16. LO 5 .... Krugman/Wells, p. 421–424, 426–427; video segment 2
    The Fed can choose open-market operations and buy bonds. This will increase the demand for bonds, causing an increase in bond prices. Increasing bond prices causes interest to decrease (Graph 1). Buying bonds also increases the money supply shown in Graph 2, which also decreases interest rates. Decreasing interest rates and increasing

money supply cause spending or aggregate demand to increase. Graph 3 illustrates the movement toward full-employment equilibrium.

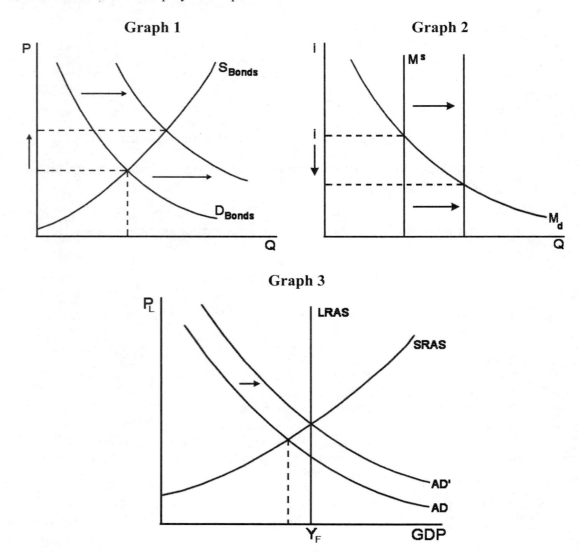

17. LO 9..................Krugman/Wells, pp. 298–299

Pessimistic business expectations will shift the investment demand curve to the left (decrease), which means even with lower interest rates, investment spending will not increase. Therefore, the aggregate demand curve will not shift toward full employment and may even decrease.

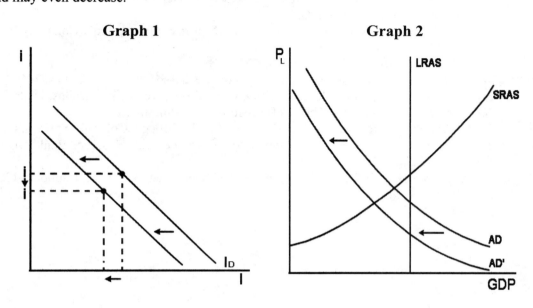

LESSON INTERVIEWEES

Michael F. Bryan, Assistant Vice-President and Economist, Applied Microeconomics Research, Federal Reserve Bank of Cleveland, Cleveland, OH

John B. Carlson, Economic Advisor, Research Department, Federal Reserve Bank of Cleveland, Cleveland, OH

Howard Hamilton, Executive Vice-President, McIlroy Bank & Trust Company, Fayetteville, AR

James A. Kornegay Jr., Tourist, Allen, TX

Wendy Lopez, President and CEO, Wendy Lopez & Associates, Inc., Dallas, TX

Robert D. McTeer Jr., President and CEO, Federal Reserve Bank of Dallas, Dallas, TX

Stephen Moore, Economist, The CATO Institute, Washington, DC

Libby Rittenberg, Professor of Economics, Colorado College, Colorado Springs, CO

Ed Stevens, Senior Consultant and Economist, Federal Reserve Bank of Cleveland, Cleveland, OH

Derek Thamm, Owner/Marketing Manager, Lubbock Feeders, L.L.C., Lubbock, TX

Lesson 11

Aggregate Expenditures

OVERVIEW

In previous lessons you have learned that $C + I + G + (X_n) = GDP$. Now we're going to look at the relationship between GDP spending (aggregate expenditures) and income at a fixed price level.

Recall that consumption is the largest component of aggregate expenditures (AE). Chapter 11 begins the AE model by developing the consumption function. The consumption function is an equation that relates consumer spending to the level of disposable income. Part of consumer spending, autonomous consumption (C_a), does not depend on income; however, most consumer spending does depend on income. Throughout this lesson the letter Y or Y_d denotes disposable income. The main part of the aggregate expenditures equation is the consumption function: $C = MPC(Y_d) + C_a$. MPC is the marginal propensity to consume and represents the percentage of an additional dollar of income that a consumer tends to spend. The remaining percentage is the marginal propensity to save (MPS). MPC + MPS always equals 1.

The next component of the AE model is planned investment (I_p). This is the part of aggregate expenditures that often has the greatest impact on the economy because it is the most volatile. Planned investment is the most volatile component since business expectations and subsequent reactions have a tremendous effect on the level of production, employment, and income in the economy. In this simplified model, planned investment does not depend on national income; therefore, it is autonomous. It is important to note that planned investment and actual investment may not be the same. Actual investment includes any unplanned changes in inventories. When adding investment to the AE model, the equation becomes $AE = MPC(Y_d) + C_a + I_p$. Any change in autonomous spending, C_a or I_p, has a multiplied effect on the macroeconomy. The simple spending multiplier = 1/MPS. By multiplying the change in autonomous spending by 1/MPS, the multiplied effect on equilibrium output and income can be calculated. Equilibrium output and income occurs when spending (AE) exactly equals the output produced in the economy.

This lesson also focuses on the investment component of aggregate expenditures and the factors that change planned investment. The video uses the roofing industry and the different businesses that contribute to a completed roof on your home to illustrate different types of investment. The video example also illustrates the multiplied effect of investment decisions on equilibrium output and income.

The last segment in the video adds net exports and government to the aggregate expenditures model. $AE = MPC(Y_d) + C_a + I_p + G + X_n$. These two components also have a multiplied effect on equilibrium income and output; however, changes in government taxing have a smaller multiplied effect than changes in government spending.

Note: In this lesson we concentrate on the AE model algebraically. The appendix to this lesson deals with the AE model graphically.

LESSON ASSIGNMENTS

Text: Krugman and Wells. *Macroeconomics*, Chapter 11, "Income and Expenditure," pp. 287–314; Chapter 12, "Aggregate Demand and Aggregate Supply," pp. 320–322, 327–329; Chapter 13, "Fiscal Policy," pp. 358–362; and Wyatt, student course guide Lesson 5 Overview

Video: "Aggregate Expenditures" from the series *Choices & Change: Macroeconomics*

LESSON OBJECTIVES

1. Describe factors that determine the amount of consumption expenditure in the economy.

2. Determine the MPC, autonomous consumption, and induced consumption from a table or equation of the consumption function.

3. Explain why shifts in consumption occur.

4. Distinguish among investment, gross private domestic investment, net private domestic investment, and depreciation.

5. Explain the rationale for the inverse relationship between investment and the interest rate.

6. Interpret an investment demand curve.

7. Identify the factors that influence the level of investment.

8. Calculate the simple spending multiplier.

9. Explain the multiplier effect.

10. Use the multiplier to solve simple problems based on changes in autonomous expenditure.

11. Define equilibrium in the aggregate expenditures model.

12. Calculate equilibrium in an aggregate expenditures model.

13. Explain the impact of a change in investment on aggregate demand and on aggregate supply.

14. Explain the effects of government spending and taxing on the AE model.

LESSON FOCUS POINTS

The following questions are designed to help you get the most benefit from the resources selected for this lesson. To maximize your learning experience:

   a. Scan the focus point questions.
   b. Read the assigned text pages.
   c. View the video.
   d. Write answers to the following questions. (References in parentheses can be used to locate information in the text and video that will help you answer the question.)

1. In terms of the consumption function, what determines consumer spending in the economy? (textbook, pp. 291–296; video segment 2)

2. If $C = .75(Y_d) + 200$, what is the marginal propensity to consume? What is autonomous consumption? What would induced consumption be if Y_d is 5,000? What is the sum of induced consumption and autonomous consumption? (textbook, pp. 291–294; video segment 2)

3. What factors cause consumption to change or shift? What factors would most likely change spending behavior? (textbook, pp. 295–296; video segment 2)

4. Define investment. What is depreciation and how does it relate to investment? (textbook, pp. 298–301; student course guide Lesson 5 Overview; video segment 3)

5. All other things held constant (*ceteris paribus*), how would businesses react to falling interest rates in the economy? (textbook, pp. 298–299; video segments 3 and 4)

6. Recreate the graph of investment demand from the video lesson and explain what causes a movement along the curve and a shift in the curve. (textbook, pp. 298–301; video segment 3)

7. According to the interviewees in the video lesson, what are the most important factors that influence the level of investment? (video segment 3)

8. Calculate the spending multiplier in the economy if consumers spend three-fourths of additional income. What happens to the multiplier if the MPC increases? (textbook, pp. 288–290; video segment 4)

9. Given the spending multiplier from the previous question and a 200 billion (200^b) increase in autonomous expenditures, create a table similar to the one for question 10 on page 313 in the Krugman textbook. Calculate the process through six rounds. (textbook, pp. 288–290, 306–309; video segment 4)

10. Calculate the potential effect on GDP and income from the 200^b increase in autonomous expenditures by using the multiplier formula. Use the information from question #8 and #9. (textbook, pp. 288–290, 306–309; video segment 4)

Lesson 11—Aggregate Expenditures

11. What is necessary for an economy to be in equilibrium? (textbook, pp. 304–306)

12. In the video, $AE = .8Y_d + 300^b + 400^b$
    $Y_d = .8Y_d + 700^b$
    $.2Y_d = 700^b$
    $Y_d = 3,500^b$
    equilibrium occurs when output, income, and spending are $3,500^b$ in the closed private economy. Calculate equilibrium if MPC increased to 90 percent. (textbook, pp. 304–306; video segment 4)

13. Due to optimistic business expectations there is an increase in investment. Graphically illustrate and explain how this would affect the aggregate demand and aggregate supply curve. (textbook, pp. 306–309; video segment 4)

14. Assuming that $AE = .75(Y_d) + 400^b + 100^b$ and government spending (G) is 200^b, calculate equilibrium income in the closed economy. What is the effect on equilibrium of adding 150^b in taxes (T)? (textbook, pp. 359–362; video segment 5)

REVIEW

The following process is intended to help you retain the knowledge you have acquired in this lesson.

- Review key points in the "Quick Reviews" at the end of each section in the textbook.
- Complete the "Check Your Understanding" questions at the end of each section and check your answers using the answer key at the end of the textbook.
- Review the case studies in "Economics in Action" in the textbook.
- Review the critical concepts noted in the page margins of the textbook.
- Complete the following Practice Test and check your responses.
- Revisit the text and/or video for any questions you answer incorrectly on the Practice Test.

PRACTICE TEST

Multiple Choice: Circle the letter that corresponds to the BEST answer for each question.

1. Household spending on goods and services is _____.
   A. taxes
   B. saving
   C. exports
   D. investment
   E. consumption

Income and Consumption

Disposable Income	Consumption
$ 100	$ 140
200	220
300	300
400	380
500	460

Use the table above to answer the following three questions.

2. When disposable income is $100, the MPC is approximately _____.
   A. 0.00
   B. 0.20
   C. 0.80
   D. 1.00
   E. 1.40

3. What is autonomous consumption?
   A. 0
   B. 20
   C. 60
   D. 300
   E. None of the above

4. What is consumption when Y_d = $1,000?
   A. $860
   B. $920
   C. $1,000
   D. $1,400
   E. None of the above

5. Given the consumption equation C = $500 + 0.8$Y_d$, if Y_d = $1,000, then induced consumption is _____.
   A. $300
   B. $500
   C. $800
   D. $1,000
   E. $1,300

6. If consumers expect their future income to decrease, the consumption function will shift _____ and savings will _____.
   A. up; increase
   B. up; decrease
   C. down; increase
   D. down; decrease
   E. down; not change

Lesson 11—Aggregate Expenditures

7. Investment is _____ spending on goods and services.
   A. foreign
   B. business
   C. household
   D. aggregate
   E. government

8. If gross private domestic investment exceeds depreciation, then _____.
   A. net private domestic investment is positive
   B. net private domestic investment is negative
   C. the capital stock is declining
   D. the capital stock is unchanged
   E. education spending is rising

9. A firm undertakes investment when _____.
   A. the stock market looks favorable
   B. it can buy plant and equipment cheaply
   C. its rate of return on capital exceeds the rate of interest or cost of funds
   D. the MPC exceeds its rate of return on capital
   E. the interest rate is higher than the rate of return on capital

Investment Projects

Project	Rate of Return	Cost
F	20%	$ 500
G	18	300
H	16	1,000
I	14	200
J	12	2,000
K	10	1,500
L	8	1,200
M	6	800

Use the table above to answer the following question.

10. If the market interest rate is 14 percent, planned investment expenditure is _____.
    A. $200
    B. $800
    C. $1,000
    D. $2,000
    E. $4,000

11. A decrease in investment demand can be caused by _____.
    A. a decrease in the market interest rate
    B. a decrease in corporate income tax rates
    C. a decrease in the cost of new capital goods
    D. a decrease in the expected demand of output
    E. an increase in the rate of new technological innovations

12. Other things remaining the same, a general decrease in the cost of new capital goods will typically _____.
    A. have no effect on the level of investment
    B. decrease total investment
    C. shift the investment demand curve to the left
    D. have no effect on the investment demand curve
    E. increase the investment demand curve

13. If the economy spends 80 percent of any increase in GDP, then an increase in investment of $1 billion results ultimately in an increase in GDP of _____.
    A. $0
    B. $0.8 billion
    C. $1.0 billion
    D. $1.8 billion
    E. $5 billion

14. The notion that a change in aggregate expenditures produces a larger change in equilibrium GDP in the aggregate expenditures model is called the _____.
    A. permanent income effect
    B. current income effect
    C. multiplier effect
    D. marginal expenditure rate
    E. marginal propensity to consume

15. In the aggregate expenditures model, equilibrium occurs if _____.
    A. consumption equals investment
    B. inventory changes equal saving
    C. inventory changes equal investment
    D. aggregate expenditures equal consumption
    E. aggregate expenditures equal GDP

Short-answer essay questions.

16. List the factors that change or shift consumption.

17. Utilize the investment demand curve below to determine investment if market interest rates are 6 percent.

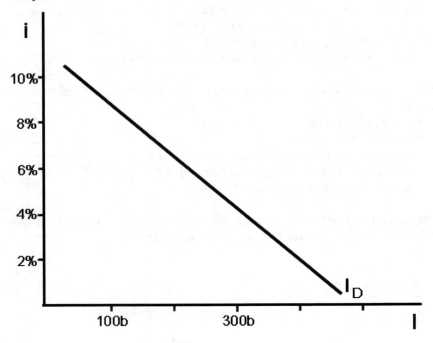

18. If $C = 0.6 Y_d + 300^b$, $I = 100^b$, $G = 50^b$ in a closed economy, calculate equilibrium income.

19. How does an increase in investment affect aggregate demand and aggregate supply?

20. Using the information in question #18, calculate the effect on equilibrium income from an increase in G of 100^b. Now in addition to the increase in G, calculate the change in equilibrium of an increase in T of 50^b.

ANSWER KEY

1. E .... LO 1 .... Krugman/Wells, p. 291; video segment 1
2. C .... LO 2 .... Krugman/Wells, pp. 292–294; video segment 2
3. C .... LO 2 .... Krugman/Wells, pp. 292–294; video segment 2
4. A .... LO 2 .... Krugman/Wells, pp. 292–294; video segment 2
5. C .... LO 2 .... Video segment 2
6. C .... LO 3 .... Krugman/Wells, pp. 295–296
7. B .... LO 4 .... Krugman/Wells, pp. 298–299; video segment 3
8. A .... LO 4 .... Wyatt, student course guide Lesson 5 Overview
9. C .... LO 5, 7 .... Krugman/Wells, pp. 298–299
10. D .... LO 7 .... Krugman/Wells, pp. 298–299
11. D .... LO 7 .... Krugman/Wells, pp. 299–301; video segment 3
12. E .... LO 7 .... Krugman/Wells, pp. 298–301; video segment 3
13. E .... LO 8, 10 ..... Krugman/Wells, pp. 288–290, 306–309; video segment 4
14. C .... LO 9 .... Krugman/Wells, pp. 288–290, 306–309; video segment 4
15. E .... LO 11 .... Krugman/Wells, pp. 304–306

Short-answer essay questions.

16. LO 1, 3 .... Krugman/Wells, pp. 295–296; video segment 2
    Consumption is the relationship between consumer spending and disposable income. Expectations and changes in real wealth will shift consumption.

17. LO 6 .... Video segment 3

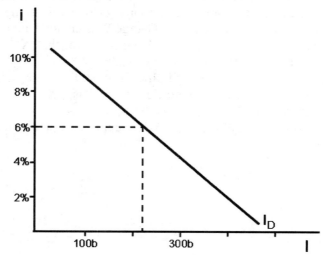

When interest rates are 6 percent, investment will be approximately 220^b, *ceteris paribus*.

Lesson 11—Aggregate Expenditures

18. LO 12.....................Krugman/Wells, pp. 304–306; video segment 4
    $Y = 0.6 Y_d + 300^b + 100^b + 50^b$
    $0.4Y = 450^b$
    $Y = 1,125^b$

19. LO 13.....................Krugman/Wells, pp. 306–309, 320–322, 327–329; video segments 3 and 4
    The increase in investment will shift AD to the right by a multiple of the investment spending. If the increase in investment is 100^b and the spending multiplier is 4, then AD shifts right 400^b. The effect on AS will depend on the type of investment. If the investment is a technological improvement or increases production capabilities, then SRAS and LRAS will increase or shift to the right.

20. LO 14.....................Krugman/Wells, pp. 358–362; video segments 4 and 5
    Previous equilibrium $Y = 1,125^b$
    The spending multiplier equals 1/.4 which equals 2.5 and if G increases 100^b, then equilibrium increases by 250^b (100^b x 2.5). The new equilibrium is $1,125^b + 250^b = 1,375^b$.
    If T increases 50^b, the tax multiplier is 1 − MPC = −1.5 and therefore, equilibrium decreases from 75^b to $1,300^b$.

LESSON INTERVIEWEES

Monty Banner, President, Ark Roofing, Inc., Irving, TX
Rhonda L. Brooks, President, Roofing Systems Business, Owens Corning, Toledo, OH
Sam F. Ciccarello, General Manager, Vigo Importing Company, Tampa, FL
Robert M. Dunn Jr., Professor of Economics, George Washington University, Washington, DC
Gus Herring, Economist, Brookhaven College, Farmers Branch, TX
Tom Motley, Professor of Art, Richland College, Dallas, TX
Louis-Paul Ricard, Sector Manager, Cargill, Inc., Tampa, FL
Chuck Sheffield, Professor of Art, Richland College, Dallas, TX
Holly St. Clair, Student, Tufts University, Medford, MA
John Yonkin, Southwest Regional Director, ABC Supply Company, Inc., Dallas, TX

Lesson 11—Appendix

Aggregate Expenditures

OVERVIEW

The aggregate expenditures model can be analyzed graphically. While there is some math involved, graphically finding equilibrium income and determining the changes to equilibrium from a spending change is often quicker than calculating it mathematically.

The graph's horizontal axis represents income and output while the vertical axis represents spending. The 45-degree (45°) line that bisects the axis represents income and spending and output combinations that are exactly in balance. This 45° line is, therefore, very useful in determining equilibrium.

The aggregate expenditures line is upward sloping with the slope being the marginal propensity to consume (MPC). The intersection of the aggregate expenditures line with the vertical axis represents autonomous spending. As investment (I_p) government (G), and net exports (X_n) are added to the model, the aggregate expenditure line will shift upwards by the amount of I_p, G, or X_n added to the model. When the consumption (C) line intersects the 45° line, then C and Y_d are equal, which represents break-even income; for example, it represents the level of income where savings (S) equals zero. The point where the C + I_p line intersects the 45° line represents an income and spending combination where savings (S) and investment (I_p) are equal. The point where the C + I_p + G line intersects with the 45° line represents equilibrium in a closed economy, that is, no foreign trade. When AE includes consumption (C), investment (I_p), government (G), and net exports (X_n), and the AE line intersects the 45° line, that point represents an equilibrium among income, spending, and output in an open economy.

LESSON ASSIGNMENTS

Text: Krugman and Wells. *Macroeconomics*, Chapter 11, "Income and Expenditure," pp. 287–314; Chapter 13, "Fiscal Policy," pp. 358–359

Video: "Aggregate Expenditures" from the series *Choices & Change: Macroeconomics*

LESSON OBJECTIVES

1. Calculate investment, net exports, and government spending using an AE graph.

2. Label equilibrium on an aggregate expenditure curve.

LESSON FOCUS POINTS

The following questions are designed to help you get the most benefit from the resources selected for this lesson. To maximize your learning experience:

a. Scan the focus point questions.
b. Read the assigned text pages.
c. View the video.
d. Write answers to the following questions. (References in parentheses can be used to locate information in the text and video that will help you answer the question.)

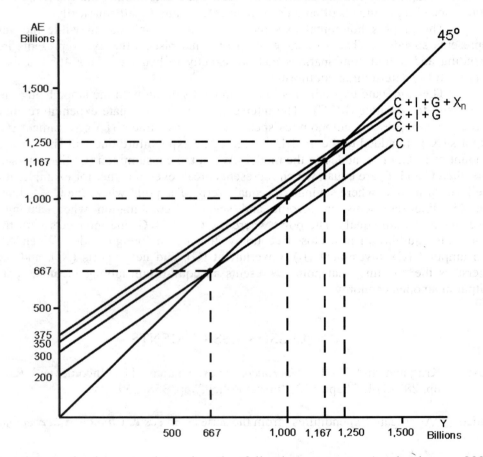

1. Use the graph above to determine the following amounts: (textbook, pp. 292–294, 303–306, 358–359; video segment 3)
   A. Autonomous consumption
   B. Autonomous investment
   C. Autonomous government
   D. Autonomous net exports
   E. Equilibrium income

2. Draw an AE curve to illustrate the example in the video. Graphically determine and label equilibrium in the "closed, private" economy. Graphically determine and label equilibrium in the "closed" economy. Graphically determine and label equilibrium in the "open" economy. (textbook, pp. 292–294, 303–306, 358–359; video segments 2 and 3)

REVIEW

The following process is intended to help you retain the knowledge you have acquired in this lesson.

- Review key points in the "Quick Reviews" at the end of each section in the textbook.
- Complete the "Check Your Understanding" questions at the end of each section and check your answers using the answer key at the end of the textbook.
- Review the case studies in "Economics in Action" in the textbook.
- Review the critical concepts noted in the page margins of the textbook.
- Complete the following Practice Test and check your responses.
- Revisit the text and/or video for any questions you answer incorrectly on the Practice Test.

PRACTICE TEST

Multiple Choice: Circle the letter that corresponds to the BEST answer for each question.

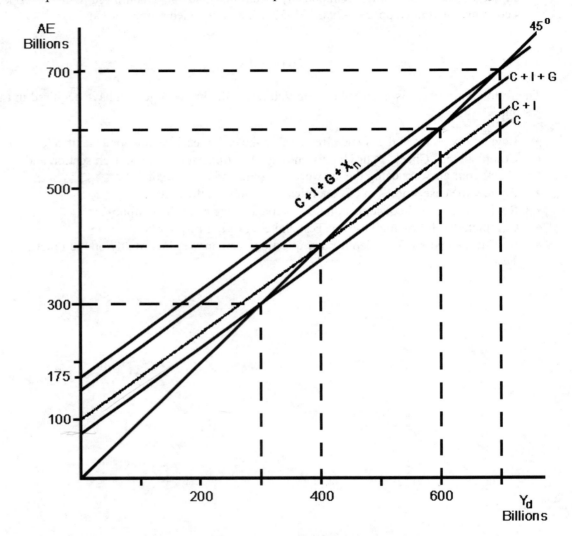

Use the graph above to answer all of the following questions.

1. Autonomous consumption is _____ billion.
   A. 0
   B. 50
   C. 75
   D. 100
   E. 300

Lesson 11: Appendix—Aggregate Expenditures

2. Break-even income is _____ billion.
   A. 75
   B. 100
   C. 300
   D. 600
   E. none of the above

3. Autonomous investment is _____ billion.
   A. 25
   B. 100
   C. 400
   D. 600
   E. none of the above

4. Autonomous government spending is _____ billion.
   A. 25
   B. 50
   C. 100
   D. 150
   E. 600

5. Net export spending is _____ billion.
   A. 25
   B. 50
   C. 150
   D. 175
   E. 700

6. Savings is equal to investment when income is _____ billion.
   A. 50
   B. 300
   C. 400
   D. 600
   E. 700

7. Equilibrium in the "closed" economy is _____ billion.
   A. 300
   B. 400
   C. 600
   D. 700
   E. none of the above

8. Equilibrium in the "open" economy is _____ billion.
   A. 300
   B. 400
   C. 600
   D. 700
   E. none of the above

Short-answer essay questions.

9. Draw the graph that represents aggregate expenditures when $C = 0.6(Y_d) + 100^b$, $I_p = 75^b$, and $G = 25^b$.

10. Illustrate on the graph drawn for question #9 an increase in government spending of 50 billion. Graphically point out the change in equilibrium income from the increase in G.

ANSWER KEY

1. C ..... LO 1 .... Krugman/Wells, pp. 292–294; video segment 2
2. C ..... LO 2 .... Wyatt, student course guide Lesson 11—Appendix Overview
3. A ..... LO 1 .... Krugman/Wells, pp. 304, 308; video segments 1 and 3
4. B ..... LO 1 .... Krugman/wells, p. 359; video segments 1 and 5
5. A ..... LO 1 .... Wyatt, student course guide Lesson 11—Appendix Overview; video segments 1 and 5
6. C ..... LO 2 .... Wyatt, student course guide Lesson 11—Appendix Overview
7. C ..... LO 2 .... Wyatt, student course guide Lesson 11—Appendix Overview
8. D ..... LO 2 .... Wyatt, student course guide Lesson 11—Appendix Overview

Short-answer essay questions.

9. LO 1, 2 ....Krugman/Wells, pp. 293, 308, 359; video segment 5

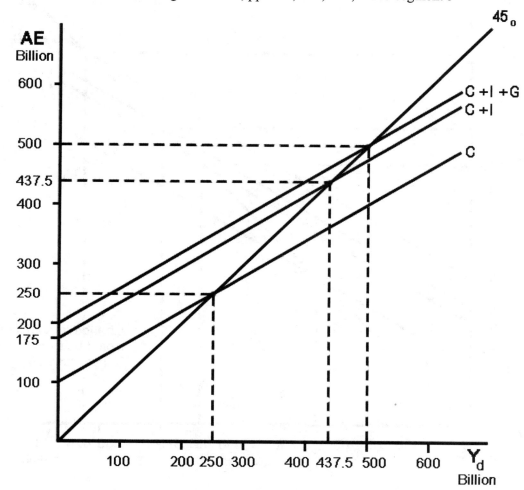

10. LO 2 ....Krugman/Wells, pp. 293, 308, 359; video segment 5

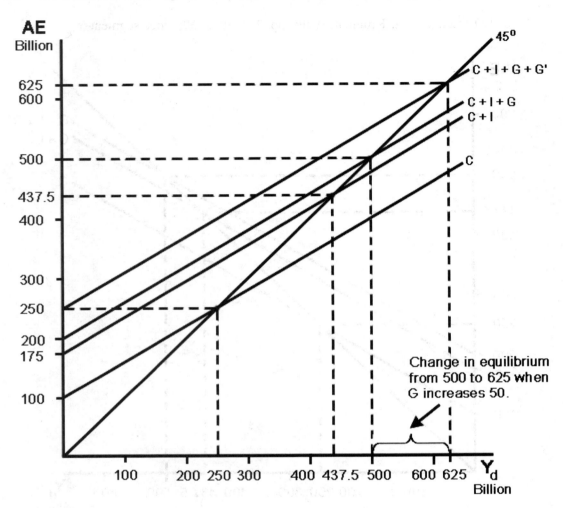

LESSON INTERVIEWEES

Monty Banner, President, Ark Roofing, Inc., Irving, TX
Rhonda L. Brooks, President, Roofing Systems Business, Owens Corning, Toledo, OH
Sam F. Ciccarello, General Manager, Vigo Importing Company, Tampa, FL
Robert M. Dunn Jr., Professor of Economics, George Washington University, Washington, DC
Gus Herring, Economist, Brookhaven College, Farmers Branch, TX
Tom Motley, Professor of Art, Richland College, Dallas, TX
Louis-Paul Ricard, Sector Manager, Cargill, Inc., Tampa, FL
Chuck Sheffield, Professor of Art, Richland College, Dallas, TX
Holly St. Clair, Student, Tufts University, Medford, MA
John Yonkin, Southwest Regional Director, ABC Supply Company, Inc., Dallas, TX

Lesson 12

Fiscal Policy

OVERVIEW

This lesson begins with a historical look at the U.S. national debt and then focuses on the effects of this debt on the macroeconomy. The national debt has often been a topic of debate, especially during election years. When this book was published, the U.S. national debt stood at nearly 5,700,000,000,000 dollars or $5.7 trillion, which is approximately $21,000 per man, woman, and child in this country. There is disagreement concerning how important the size of the debt is, as well as disagreement over who actually bears the burden of paying the debt. Is this level of debt a major concern for our economy? Opinions are quite varied on this subject. Make a note of your opinion on the subject prior to reading the rest of the material and viewing the video.

The third segment focuses on the fiscal policies during the Ronald Reagan administration and the development and use of supply-side economic theory. Some of Reagan's proposals were based on Arthur Laffer's work. The Laffer curve represents the relationship between marginal tax rates and tax revenue received by the government. If the government sets the marginal tax rate to the right of the curve's peak, then a decrease in tax rates leads to an increase in tax revenue. The major tax cuts during the Reagan administration were aimed at increasing the incentives to work, save, and invest. If taxpayers were to receive more of the income they earned, this in turn was supposed to cause tax revenues to rise. Again, there is disagreement over the validity of such an argument. Included in this segment are the compounding effects on the national debt of major tax cuts and increased military spending during the 1980s.

The last segment presents the fiscal policies and promises of the Bush and Clinton administrations in the 1990s and the effects on economic growth and the national debt. One of the most important concepts in this lesson is that the state of the economy, good or bad, is often a result of the actions or inaction of a past president, his administration, and particularly of Congress. Praising or blaming a current administration for the state of the economy is often undeserved.

LESSON ASSIGNMENTS

Text: Krugman and Wells. *Macroeconomics*, Chapter 10, "Savings, Investment Spending, and the Financial System," pp. 258–260; Chapter 13, "Fiscal Policy," pp. 351–380

Video: "Fiscal Policy" from the series *Choices & Change: Macroeconomics*

LESSON OBJECTIVES

1. Distinguish between the following pairs: government purchases and government spending, and expansionary and contractionary fiscal policies.

2. Explain the difference between the deficit and the debt.

3. Explain how changes in the following affect aggregate expenditures: personal income taxes, transfer payments, business taxes, payroll taxes, and government purchases.

4. Utilize AS/AD curves to illustrate fiscal policy effects.

LESSON FOCUS POINTS

The following questions are designed to help you get the most benefit from the resources selected for this lesson. To maximize your learning experience:

    a. Scan the focus point questions.
    b. Read the assigned text pages.
    c. View the video.
    d. Write answers to the following questions. (References in parentheses can be used to locate information in the text and video that will help you answer the question.)

1. List two examples of government purchases and two examples of government spending that are not purchases. How do these differ? (textbook, pp. 353–354)

2. List two examples of expansionary fiscal policy and two examples of contractionary fiscal policy. Describe how these examples will work to expand or contract the economy. (textbook, pp. 355–356)

3. Use the AS/AD model to illustrate the effects of the expansionary and contractionary fiscal policy examples from question #2. Highlight the effects on equilibrium price levels and equilibrium output levels. (textbook, pp. 355–356)

4. Explain why some federal deficits are unavoidable. Compare a deficit created when an economy is in a recession to a deficit created when an economy is expanding. What is the importance of the difference? (textbook, pp. 363–367)

5. How does the federal government create the national debt? (textbook, pp. 368–373; video segment 2)

6. Aggregate expenditures are equal to $C+I_g+G+X_n$. What happens to AE when there are increases in each of the following: personal income taxes, transfer payments, business taxes, and government purchases? (textbook, pp. 355–356)

Lesson 12—Fiscal Policy

REVIEW

The following process is intended to help you retain the knowledge you have acquired in this lesson.

- Review key points in the "Quick Reviews" at the end of each section in the textbook.
- Complete the "Check Your Understanding" questions at the end of each section and check your answers using the answer key at the end of the textbook.
- Review the case studies in "Economics in Action" in the textbook.
- Review the critical concepts noted in the page margins of the textbook.
- Complete the following Practice Test and check your responses.
- Revisit the text and/or video for any questions you answer incorrectly on the Practice Test.

PRACTICE TEST

Multiple Choice: Circle the letter that corresponds to the BEST answer for each question.

1. Public investment expenditure for highways, schools, and national defense is included in _____ purchases.
   A. household
   B. investment
   C. government
   D. consumption
   E. net export

2. Expansionary fiscal policy includes _____.
   A. decreasing taxes
   B. increasing taxes
   C. decreasing the money supply
   D. increasing the money supply
   E. decreasing government expenditures

3. Contractionary fiscal policy includes _____.
   A. decreasing taxes
   B. decreasing the money supply
   C. increasing the money supply
   D. decreasing government expenditures
   E. increasing government expenditures

4. If the government's total revenue is greater than total expenditures, then it has a budget _____.
   A. deficit
   B. surplus
   C. balance
   D. equality
   E. equilibrium

5. A deficit _____.
   A. exists when government revenues exceed government spending
   B. is the sum of all past government spending less any repayments
   C. only occurs when an economy is in a recession
   D. exists when government spending exceeds government revenue
   E. none of the above

6. Transfer payments _____.
   A. typically rise during expansionary periods
   B. typically fall during recessions
   C. do not change as the economy expands and contracts during the business cycle
   D. fall during expansionary periods and rise during contractionary periods
   E. have no impact, one way or another, on the level of expenditures

7. If the federal government increases purchases, then a likely result is _____.
   A. an increase in real GDP
   B. a decrease in consumption
   C. an increase in unemployment
   D. a decrease in the price level
   E. a decrease in aggregate demand

8. If the federal government increases income taxes, then a likely result is _____.
   A. an increase in real GDP
   B. an increase in consumption
   C. a decrease in unemployment
   D. a decrease in the price level
   E. a increase in aggregate demand

9. The _____ curve suggests that at some level of taxation, a decrease in business taxes could actually lead to an increase in government tax revenue.
   A. Laffer
   B. investment demand
   C. aggregate supply
   D. aggregate demand
   E. Phillips

10. If the economy is in a recessionary gap, an appropriate fiscal policy response might include _____.
    A. an increase in taxes
    B. a decrease in the discount rate
    C. a decrease in unemployment benefits
    D. the purchase of government bonds
    E. an increase in government spending on roads and bridges

11. _____ is an example of an implicit liability of the United States government.
    A. Revenue received from income taxes
    B. Social Security
    C. Government spending on education
    D. Interest paid on the national debt
    E. Government spending on national defense

Short-answer essay questions.

12. Compare your pre-lesson opinion on the national debt with your after-lesson opinion.

13. Explain the difference in the deficit and the debt in terms of personal finance.

14. Draw an AS/AD graph to illustrate the effect from question #7.

15. Draw an AS/AD graph to illustrate the effect from question #8.

16. Based on the video "Fiscal Policy," graphically illustrate the effects on the macroeconomy from actions taken during the Reagan administration.

17. Based on the video "Fiscal Policy," graphically illustrate the effects on the macroeconomy from the actions taken to reduce the deficit during the George H.W. Bush administration (1988-1992).

ANSWER KEY

1. C .... LO 1 .... Krugman/Wells, pp. 353–354
2. A .... LO 1 .... Krugman/Wells, pp. 355–356
3. D .... LO 1 .... Krugman/Wells, pp. 355–356
4. B .... LO 2 .... Krugman/Wells, p. 259; video segment 2
5. D .... LO 2 .... Krugman/Wells, p. 259; video segment 2
6. D .... LO 3 .... Krugman/Wells, pp. 363–366
7. A .... LO 3 .... Krugman/Wells, p. 355
8. D .... LO 3 .... Krugman/Wells, pp. 355–356; video segment 3
9. A .... LO 3 .... Video segment 3
10. E .... LO 1 .... Krugman/Wells, pp. 355–356
11. B .... LO 1, 2 .... Krugman/Wells, pp. 372–373

Short-answer essay questions.

12. LO 2........................Krugman/Wells, pp. 368–372; video segment 2
    Answers will vary.

13. LO 2........................Krugman/Wells, pp. 368–370; video segment 2
    When you spend more dollars than your income in a given time period, then you incur a deficit. The borrowing to pay for the spending that exceeds income added to past borrowing less any reductions or payments on the debt represents total debt. Borrowing includes credit card balances which are part of consumer debt.

14. LO 4........................Krugman/Wells, p. 355

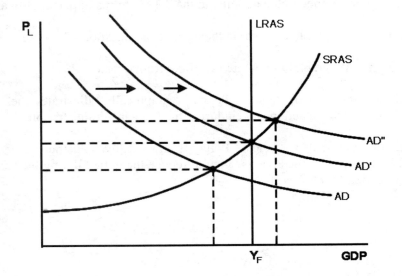

An increase in government purchases will shift AD to the right. If the economy was experiencing a recessionary gap, then the increase to AD' would close the recessionary gap. If the economy was at full employment and AD' shifted to AD", then an inflationary gap would be created.

15. LO 4........................Krugman/Wells, pp. 355–356; video segment 3

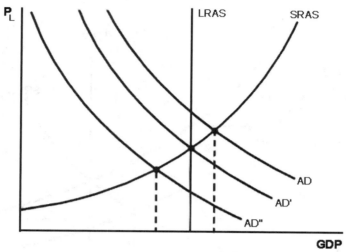

An increase in income taxes would cause a decrease in AD since consumers would have less income to spend. If the economy was experiencing an inflationary gap, then the decrease in AD would bring the economy back toward full-employment equilibrium. If the economy was at full employment or experiencing a recessionary gap, then the decrease in AD would either cause a recession or deepen the existing recession.

16. LO 4........................Krugman/Wells, pp. 355–356; video segment 3

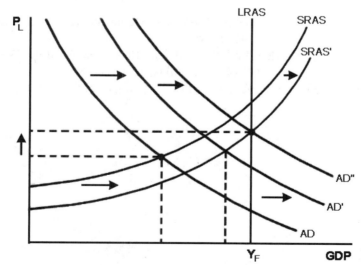

The tax cuts were supposed to increase both aggregate supply and aggregate demand. There were also some major increases in government spending on the military. This also increased aggregate demand.

Lesson 12—Fiscal Policy

17. LO 4.........................Krugman/Wells, pp. 355–356; video segment 4
President Bush's tax increases caused a decrease in aggregate demand and higher rates of unemployment.

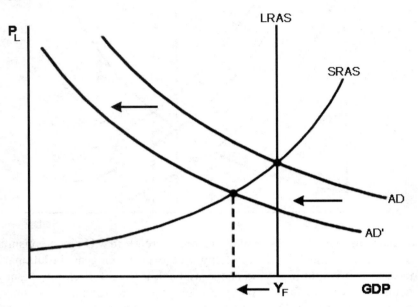

LESSON INTERVIEWEES

Frank Ackerman, Research Assistant Professor, Department of Urban and Environmental Policy, Tufts University, Medford, MA
Diana Furchgott-Roth, Resident Fellow, American Enterprise Institute, Washington, DC
Philip Seib, Political Analyst, WFAA-TV, Dallas, TX
Timothy Tregarthen, Economist/Author, University of Colorado, Colorado Springs, CO

Lesson 13

Schools of Thought

OVERVIEW

The evolution of economic thought is as dynamic as the macroeconomy that it tries to explain. This lesson deals with the major macroeconomic theories that have influenced government decisions for the past 100 years. Remember from Lesson 4 that economies go through phases of the business cycle, alternating between periods of expansion and contraction.

Prior to the Great Depression, classical economic theory was generally accepted in the United States as explaining how an economy works. In this theory, if an economy is experiencing either an inflationary or a recessionary period, then flexible wages, prices, and interest rates will adjust to bring the economy back to full-employment equilibrium. Classical economics adequately explained the behavior of the economy until the Great Depression, when some things seemed to change. Classical economists argued that actions taken by the government and Federal Reserve intensified the Depression and that if the government had not disrupted the adjustment process, then the Depression would not have been so severe. The second segment looks further at the disagreement over the causes as well as the "cure" for the Great Depression.

The third segment continues with a historical view of macroeconomic theory from post–World War II through the Reagan administration in the 1980s. During this period, the Phillips curve was developed to represent the inverse relationship between unemployment and inflation. The Phillips curve theory held until the United States experienced a period of *stagflation*, which is simultaneous high unemployment and high inflation. This period led to *supply-side* economic theory, which is often referred to as "Reaganomics." "Trickle-down," which is another way of expressing a multiplier effect, was an expression sometimes used to refer to Reaganomics. In other words, government actions to stimulate economic activity and, at the same time, lower inflation rates, were meant to flow through the economy down to the lower income levels. This was to be accomplished by cutting marginal tax rates to stimulate working, saving, and investment and, therefore, to create jobs. Recall from Lesson 12 that the idea of cutting marginal tax rates came from Arthur Laffer, who argued that tax rates were too high. In his opinion, if the government cut tax rates, the effect would be to increase the incentive to work more since less of the income would go to the government. Laffer also argued that decreased tax rates and increased work would cause government tax revenues to rise. This segment also looks at how successful supply-side theory was in the 1980s.

The focus of the last segment is economic theory in the last decade of the twentieth century. For the most part, the economy grew and expanded while keeping inflation very low, once again violating the logic of the fixed Phillips curve. The Federal Reserve's policies have been both credited and criticized during this period.

LESSON ASSIGNMENTS

Text: Krugman and Wells. *Macroeconomics*, Chapter 9, "Long-Run Economic Growth," pp. 230–242, and Chapter 11, "Income and Expenditure," pp. 298–299; Chapter 12, "Aggregate Demand and Aggregate Supply," pp. 336–338; Chapter 15, "Monetary Policy," pp. 432–433; Chapter 16, "Inflation, Disinflation, and Deflation," pp. 443–468; Chapter 17, "Macroeconomics: Events and Ideas," pp. 469–491

Video: "Schools of Thought" from the series *Choices & Change: Macroeconomics*

LESSON OBJECTIVES

1. Explain why unemployment and inflation may rise or fall together at times, while at other times they move in opposite directions.

2. Explain why the long-run cause of inflation is generally agreed to be excessive monetary growth.

3. Discuss disagreements over the monetary policy actions of the Fed.

4. Explain the relationship between the output gap and cyclical unemployment.

5. Evaluate the likely impact on growth from a proposed set of policy actions.

6. Explain the relationship between saving and economic growth.

7. Describe the differences and similarities in the basic beliefs of monetarists and new classicals.

8. Predict policy positions of the different schools of economic thought in dealing with economic problems.

LESSON FOCUS POINTS

The following questions are designed to help you get the most benefit from the resources selected for this lesson. To maximize your learning experience:

    a. Scan the focus point questions.
    b. Read the assigned text pages.
    c. View the video.
    d. Write answers to the following questions. (References in parentheses can be used to locate information in the text and video that will help you answer the question.)

1. The Phillips curve model suggests there is a tradeoff between inflation and unemployment. What are the reasons for this tradeoff? (textbook, pp. 451–457; video segment 3)

2. Stagflation is simultaneous high inflation and high unemployment. What are the causes of stagflation? What is the cure for stagflation? (textbook, pp. 336–338; video segment 3)

3. How does excessive monetary growth affect the macroeconomy? (textbook, pp. 432–433, 444–446, 472–474, 476–479; video segment 4)

4. The Fed has been regarded as the guardian against inflation. The Fed is also an independent government agency whose primary purpose is to promote economic stability. In the video "Schools of Thought," what are the common criticisms leveled against the Fed? (video segment 4)

5. What are expansionary monetary and fiscal policies? When are they used and what do they entail? What will happen to output levels when they are used? What will happen to the level of spending in the economy when they are used? (textbook, pp. 355–356, 426–427, 484–486; video segment 2)

6. What are contractionary monetary and fiscal policies? When are they used and what do they entail? What will happen to the level of spending in the economy when they are used? (textbook, pp. 355–356, 426–427; video segment 4)

7. Economic growth can be defined as increases in real GDP over time. Briefly explain some economic policies that facilitate or promote economic growth. (textbook, pp. 230–242; video segment 4)

8. Savings is a prerequisite for investment and provides funds that can be made available for producing capital goods. How do savings and investments affect economic growth? (textbook, p. 238; video segments 3 and 4)

9. What are the basic beliefs of the monetarist school of economics? How does monetarism compare to the basic beliefs of the new classical school of economics? (textbook, pp. 476–483; video segment 4)

10. Briefly outline the different policy positions for the various macroeconomic theories or schools of thought in regard to reducing inflation and unemployment rates. (textbook, pp. 470–488; video segments 3, 4, and 5)

11. Explain and differentiate between the following terms: *Okun's law, rational expectations, the natural rate hypothesis, real business cycle theory, the political business cycle, liquidity trap,* and *zero bound.* (textbook, pp. 453, 463–465, 476–484)

REVIEW

The following process is intended to help you retain the knowledge you have acquired in this lesson.

- Review key points in the "Quick Reviews" at the end of each section in the textbook.
- Complete the "Check Your Understanding" questions at the end of each section and check your answers using the answer key at the end of the textbook.
- Review the case studies in "Economics in Action" in the textbook.
- Review the critical concepts noted in the page margins of the textbook.
- Complete the following Practice Test and check your responses.
- Revisit the text and/or video for any questions you answer incorrectly on the Practice Test.

PRACTICE TEST

Multiple Choice: Circle the letter that corresponds to the BEST answer for each question.

1. Suppose the economy experiences an increase in the unemployment rate at the same time the inflation rate declines. This situation indicates a _____.
    A. shift in the short-run Phillips curve
    B. movement along the vertical long-run Phillips curve
    C. movement along the horizontal long-run Phillips curve
    D. movement along the positively sloped short-run Phillips curve
    E. movement along the negatively sloped short-run Phillips curve

2. Other things remaining the same, an economy is better off on _____.
    A. the highest possible Phillips curve
    B. the top left of a given Phillips curve
    C. the bottom right of a given Phillips curve
    D. a lower Phillips curve than a higher Phillips curve
    E. a higher Phillips curve than a lower Phillips curve

3. In the 1970s, the U.S. economy _____.
    A. shifted to a lower Phillips curve
    B. shifted to a higher Phillips curve
    C. moved along a short-run Phillips curve
    D. moved along a long-run Phillips curve
    E. exhibited no tradeoff between unemployment and inflation

4. The short-run Phillips curve would shift up due to _____.
    A. a decrease in the actual rate of inflation
    B. an increase in the actual rate of inflation
    C. a decrease in the expected rate of inflation
    D. an increase in the expected rate of inflation
    E. a decrease in the natural rate of unemployment

5. Stagflation is explained by shifts to the _____.
   A. right in the SRAS curve
   B. left in the SRAS curve
   C. right in the LRAS curve
   D. left in the AD curve
   E. right in the AD curve

6. _____ exists when monetary policy is NOT effective because nominal interest rates are at the zero bound.
   A. A recessionary gap
   B. An inflationary gap
   C. An output gap
   D. Hyperinflation
   E. A liquidity trap

7. According to Okun's law, there is a(n) _____ relationship between the output gap and _____.
   A. indeterminate; the employment rate
   B. negative; cyclical employment
   C. positive; price level
   D. negative; the inflation rate
   E. nonexistent; cyclical unemployment

8. Fiscal and monetary policy can be used to promote economic growth by _____.
   A. decreasing interest rates
   B. discouraging savings
   C. reducing spending on infrastructure
   D. expanding the federal budget surplus
   E. increasing unemployment

9. Fiscal and monetary policy can be used to promote economic growth by _____.
   A. increasing interest rates
   B. discouraging savings
   C. increasing spending on infrastructure
   D. expanding the federal budget surplus
   E. increasing unemployment

10. In general, an economy that saves more today will _____.
    A. show an increase in consumption today
    B. show a decrease in consumption in the future
    C. be able to produce less real output in the future
    D. be able to produce more real output in the future
    E. cause the production possibilities curve to shift inward

11. New classical economics is based on the proposition that _____.
    A. prices and wages are sticky
    B. output seldom achieves full employment
    C. business cycles are good for the economy
    D. people make logically reasoned forecasts from existing information
    E. changes in the money supply have a direct impact on changes in the price level

12. New classical economics contends that policy activism is _____.
    A. not warranted because we do not know enough about the workings of the economy to stabilize it
    B. not warranted because the public defeats discretionary policies since everyone expects them, and therefore, their effectiveness is thwarted
    C. not warranted since discretionary policies have no effect on real output
    D. warranted because expectations are rational only in the short run
    E. warranted because expectations are rational only in the long run

13. The ability of the economy to adjust its natural level of employment on its own _____.
    A. would bring about an increasing role in government fiscal policy
    B. would bring about an increasing role in the Federal Reserve's monetary policy
    C. would have a major impact on U.S. international trade policy
    D. is the heart of a fundamental disagreement among economists about the role of public policy
    E. is an issue addressed by economists

14. The theory that business cycles are partially caused by "animal spirits" was advocated by _____.
    A. Ben Bernanke
    B. John Maynard Keynes
    C. Milton Friedman
    D. Adam Smith
    E. David Ricardo

15. The assertion that an economy with steady growth in the money supply will experience steady growth in GDP is associated with _____.
    A. classical economic theory
    B. monetarism
    C. Keynesian economic theory
    D. the political business cycle
    E. the classical economic theory

16. _____ suggests that setting policy to achieve an unemployment rate below the natural rate will lead to a continual increase in the rate of inflation.
    A. Okun's law
    B. The Phillips curve
    C. The natural rate hypothesis
    D. Monetarism
    E. Real business cycle theory

Short-answer essay question.

17. From the video "Schools of Thought," characterize the different opinions concerning active monetary policy carried out by the Federal Reserve.

ANSWER KEY

1. E .... LO 1 .... Krugman/Wells, pp. 453–456; video segment 3
2. D .... LO 1 .... Krugman/Wells, pp. 453–457; video segment 3
3. B .... LO 1 .... Krugman/Wells, pp. 457–458; video segment 3
4. D .... LO 1 .... Krugman/Wells, pp. 453–457; video segment 3
5. B .... LO 1 .... Krugman/Wells, pp. 336–338; video segment 3
6. E .... LO 3 .... Krugman/Wells, pp. 463–464
7. B .... LO 4 .... Krugman/Wells, p. 453
8. A .... LO 5 .... Krugman/Wells, pp. 238, 298–299; video segments 2 and 3
9. C .... LO 5 .... Krugman/Wells, pp. 240–241; video segments 2 and 3
10. D .... LO 6 .... Krugman/Wells, p. 238
11. D .... LO 7 .... Krugman/Wells, pp. 481–482
12. B .... LO 7 .... Krugman/Wells, pp. 481–482
13. D .... LO 8 .... Krugman/Wells, pp. 484–488
14. B .... LO 8 .... Krugman/Wells, pp. 472–474
15. B .... LO 8 .... Krugman/Wells, pp. 477–478
16. C .... LO 8 .... Krugman/Wells, p. 479

Short-answer essay question.

17. LO 3 .... video segment 4
    Some argue that the Fed's actions cause many of our macroeconomic problems. For example, during the Great Depression, many banks were allowed to fail and the money supply decreased. The Fed also increased the reserve ratio. These actions turned what could have been a long recession into the Great Depression.
    Today, there is disagreement over whether the Fed should engage in active monetary policy. For the most part, there seems to be agreement that inflation is primarily a monetary phenomenon. Whether monetary policy can strongly affect economic activity is still debated.

LESSON INTERVIEWEES

Jeff Carbiener, Adjunct Professor of Economics, Southern Methodist University, Dallas, TX
John B. Carlson, Economic Advisor, Research Department, Federal Reserve Bank of Cleveland, Cleveland, OH
Robert D. McTeer Jr., President and CEO, Federal Reserve Bank of Dallas, Dallas, TX
Ester-Mirjam Sent, Assistant Professor, University of Notre Dame, Notre Dame, IN

Lesson 14

Economies in Transition

OVERVIEW

Market capitalism and command socialism are extremes of the economic spectrum. All economic systems have elements of both capitalism and socialism; that is, there are varying degrees of socialism mixed into capitalist systems and vice versa. The most significant difference between capitalism and socialism is the ownership or control of productive resources. Economic systems usually evolve slowly over time, but sometimes there are violent upheavals. This lesson looks at examples of both changes.

One problem associated with command systems is the inability to react to shortages in a timely manner. Since command systems rely on central planning rather than incentives, inefficiency is often rampant. In contrast, market economies have a profit incentive that leads to quick elimination of shortages and surpluses. Also, risk taking and innovations occur in market economies because of the potential rewards for success.

The video examines Japan as one example of a market capitalist country with a significant level of government involvement in the economy. At the beginning of the twenty-first century, Japan was characterized by few natural resources, major import barriers, and cooperation between business and government. Japan has had a system where occupations and careers have often been predetermined by tradition. This segment also illustrates the brief history of the Soviet Union, which was created in the violent Russian Revolution of 1917. Following the revolution, the Soviet Union became the premier example of a command economy where the government decided how productive resources would be used and how output would be distributed. This was an extremely difficult task considering the Soviet Union was geographically over twice the size of the United States with enormous amounts of productive resources. This segment also explores the varying levels of government involvement in the economy in other countries, including the United States.

The third segment presents an interesting social experiment that was very successful in helping Israel increase its productive capacity and standard of living. The Kibbutzim, which began in the early 1900s, were instrumental in the survival of Israel. They turned a barren, rock-laden desert into a productive agrarian base. More recently, the Kibbutzim have expanded into manufacturing and tourism.

The evolution of the Cuban economy is the focus of the last segment. After centuries of Spanish rule, Cuba became independent with the aid of the United States. In the late 1950s, Cuba became a command-based economy with the takeover by Fidel Castro. The success of Castro's regime was due in large part to aid from the Soviet Union. When the Soviet Union dissolved, Cuba lost a major supporter. Now, Cuba must try to maintain its economy without massive aid.

All economic systems are combinations of market capitalism and command socialism, and macroeconomies continue to experiment, change, and evolve.

LESSON ASSIGNMENTS

Text: Krugman and Wells. *Macroeconomics*, Chapter 9, "Long-Run Economic Growth," pp. 225–256; Wyatt, student course guide Lesson 2 Overview

Video: "Economies in Transition" from the series *Choices & Change: Macroeconomics*

LESSON OBJECTIVES

1. Define market (capitalist) and command types of economic systems.

2. Examine socialism in action.

3. Explore the history of utopian societies.

4. Explore some of the economic successes and failures of countries that have experienced major changes in their economic focus.

LESSON FOCUS POINTS

The following questions are designed to help you get the most benefit from the resources selected for this lesson. To maximize your learning experience:

    a. Scan the focus point questions.
    b. Read the assigned text pages.
    c. View the video.
    d. Write answers to the following questions. (References in parentheses can be used to locate information in the text and video that will help you answer the question.)

1. Use examples from the video "Economies in Transition" to explain how market capitalism differs from command socialism. (video segment 2)

2. Utilize information from the textbook and video to present an argument for or against command socialism based on the successes and failures. (textbook, pp. 225–256; video segments 2, 3, and 4)

3. What are some of the problems associated with Cuba's loss of Soviet aid? What is the country doing to survive the loss? (video segment 4)

4. Compare the Kibbutz concept to Marxian ideas. (video segment 3)

5. Name some countries that have experienced major changes in economic focus. In other words, what countries have undergone fundamental changes in regard to owning property resources and how resources are allocated? Briefly comment on their experience with these changes. (video segments 2 and 4)

REVIEW

The following process is intended to help you retain the knowledge you have acquired in this lesson.

- Review key points in the "Quick Reviews" at the end of each section in the textbook.
- Complete the "Check Your Understanding" questions at the end of each section and check your answers using the answer key at the end of the textbook.
- Review the case studies in "Economics in Action" in the textbook.
- Review the critical concepts noted in the page margins of the textbook.
- Complete the following Practice Test and check your responses.
- Revisit the text and/or video for any questions you answer incorrectly on the Practice Test.

PRACTICE TEST

Multiple Choice: Circle the letter that corresponds to the BEST answer for each question.

1. An economic system in which most capital is privately owned and allocative decisions are made by the private sector is _____.
   A. market commandism
   B. command socialism
   C. market socialism
   D. command capitalism
   E. market capitalism

2. Countries with the highest average standard of living follow _____.
   A. market commandism
   B. command socialism
   C. market socialism
   D. command capitalism
   E. market capitalism

3. In the late twentieth century, Japan was characterized by _____.
   A. abundant mineral resources
   B. very little cooperation between business and government
   C. high barriers to imports
   D. a civil service system that is independent of business
   E. low per capita production

4. In the late twentieth century, Japan was characterized by _____.
   A. abundant mineral resources
   B. extensive cooperation between business and government
   C. almost no barriers to imports
   D. a civil service system that is independent of business
   E. low per capita production

5. The economy of Sweden is characterized by _____.
   A. limited income redistribution programs
   B. historically low living standards
   C. very little government involvement in the economy
   D. high tax rates
   E. indicative planning

6. Centrally controlled economies had moderate success in achieving the goals of _____.
   A. equity and growth
   B. equity and stability
   C. growth and stability
   D. efficiency and growth
   E. efficiency and stability

7. An evaluation of centrally planned economies reveals that they have _____.
   A. put a premium on technological innovation
   B. achieved a nearly equal distribution of income
   C. been successful in attaining economic efficiency
   D. experienced production rigidities and shortages
   E. experienced higher rates of inflation than most capitalist countries

8. Central control proved to be a failure in communist countries because of _____.
   A. abundant market information
   B. unquestioned reliance on the price system
   C. excessive incentives for economic growth
   D. insufficient use of government ownership
   E. inadequate rewards for innovation

Short-answer essay questions.

9. Briefly describe the attempts at utopian societies presented in the video "Economies in Transition."

10. Explain where a Kibbutz falls in the economic spectrum between socialism and market capitalism.

ANSWER KEY

1. E .... LO 1 .... Wyatt, telecourse guide Lesson 2 Overview; video segment 2
2. E .... LO 1 .... Krugman/Wells, pp. 226–228; video segment 2
3. C .... LO 2 .... Wyatt, student course guide Lesson 14 Overview
4. B .... LO 2 .... Wyatt, student course guide Lesson 14 Overview; video segment 2
5. D .... LO 2 .... video segment 2
6. B .... LO 4 .... video segments 2 and 4
7. D .... LO 4 .... Wyatt, student course guide Lesson 14 Overview
8. E .... LO 4 .... Wyatt, student course guide Lesson 14 Overview

Short-answer essay questions.

9. LO 3 .... video segment 3

    The concept of a utopian society has been around for thousands of years. The French revolution and later the Russian revolution were driven by the desire of many to have a more equitable system. "Hippie" communes in the United States were based on utopian ideas. The video highlights one of the most successful attempts at a utopian society, the Kibbutz.

10. LO 1, 4 .... video segment 3

    The Kibbutz system is very unusual. It is based on the Marxian concept of contributing what you can and only taking what you need. What's left is used to expand the community. What's unusual is this very socialist ideal is governed in a very democratic manner. Everything is done for the good of the community, but it is the individuals in the community that make the decisions by democratic voting.

LESSON INTERVIEWEES

Steven L. Cobb, Chair, Department of Economics, University of North Texas, Denton, TX
Barry L. Duman, Ph.D., Professor of Economics, West Texas A&M University, Canyon, TX
Luis Locay, Associate Professor, University of Miami, Coral Gables, FL
Annette Morganstern, Director, American Zionist Movement, Dallas, TX
David L. Ramsour, President, Texas Council on Economic Education, Houston, TX
Jorge A. Sanguinetty, President, DevTech Systems, Inc., International Economic Consultant, Washington, DC